The Complete Guide to
Ally McBeal

Louis Chunovic

B🍂XTREE

First published in 1999 by Boxtree, an imprint of Macmillan Publishers Ltd, 25 Eccleston Place, London SW1W 9NF, Basingstoke and Oxford.

Associated companies throughout the world.

www.macmillan.co.uk

ISBN 0 7522 1332 6

Text © Macmillan Publishers Ltd, 1999

9 8 7 6 5 4 3

A CIP catalogue record for this book is available from the British Library.

Designed and typeset by Ben Cracknell Studios
Colour reproduction by Aylesbury Studios
Printed in Great Britain by Mackays of Chatham

The Complete Guide to
Ally McBeal

Contents

The First Season 93

The Second Season 145

To The Reader

I've written this sort of book before, Gentle Reader, something for fans of a hot new show. Generally, I enjoy it, invariably learning things as well in the process, and trying to give honest value to the reader by telling what I know. This time, this book is not authorized, although it's essentially the same one I'd have produced if commissioned by the network or studio. (I like to think the result is essentially the same, that I still tell you what I know and what I think about what I've learned when the book is authorized, but ultimately that's for others to decide.)

There are a number of stories in this book, both real and fictional. But one of the most fascinating, to me, is the one about the serious young New York stage actress who was plucked up by television and became wildly successful, a transatlantic pop-culture phenomenon of the first magnitude. With TV success came, perhaps inevitably, the intense and uncaring press speculation, carelessly intrusive and often masking its prurient interest as concern. The Germans have a word for it – *schadenfreude* – and under its sickly colour Calista Flockhart has suffered the worst prying indignities of sudden tabloid-style fame.

This is a book written on the fly, in more ways than one, and it suffers thereby from some unavoidable defects. I've drawn both on my own experiences, covering and working in television, and on the work of other writers and journalists, particularly those who've interviewed Ms Flockhart during the past two media-firestorm years. I'm impressed by how well they've handled an apparently difficult (though understandably so) interview subject and a certainly difficult subject matter, splashed across the tabloids as it was, touching on many of the 'hot button' social issues of the day. They've almost invariably shed light even as, perforce, they've added heat to the fire. Much of this book's merit comes from their original work, which I've analysed and often reinterpreted with the benefit of some hindsight. For the book's defects: *mea culpa*. But that's all right – appropriate, too.

That's because 'on the fly' is quite obviously the way the gifted David E. Kelley works. He writes every *Ally* script, and many of the scripts for his other shows too, and he reportedly turns out a new one every four days.

Take it from a professional writer who knows a thing or two about TV: this is an awesome pace and an awesome output, and it's all at a rather dazzling level of quality.

So my thanks to the prolific Mr Kelley. Without him none of what follows would exist.

Calista, Kelley, the Press and the Show

Food Fight

It was a balmy summer's eve, the weekend before the annual celebration of American independence (from a certain unnamed though no doubt still culturally superior nation), and there was The Actress, on a chat show on late-night national television, having a little independence celebration herself, after a long and sometimes quite nasty season of gossip and mean speculation.

From its very beginning her show had been a pop-cultural lightning rod, sparking brush fires about everything from the end of feminism to the revival of the miniskirt, and becoming the focus of endless media debate about the trials (both real and figurative) of women, particularly those who were young and single, in the post-modern workplace.

And as if the character she played wasn't controversial enough (was she a feminist ideal or a male fantasy? competent or clumsy? empowered or needy and dependent on men for her self-esteem? and so on and so on), speculation had grown about The Actress herself as well.

That speculation – about the state of her physical well-being and, well, to put it bluntly, the state of her mental health – had burned quietly in gossipy Hollywood insider conversations at pricey Beverly Hills expense-account restaurants since the show's debut. That was the way it went in Tinseltown, though, where fear of high-profile failure bred not only wholesale imitation but rampant professional jealousies as well. Sometimes the insider gossip was true, but even more often – and this is an important point – it was not.

In any case, the insider rumour and innuendo erupted into a full-on firestorm of public controversy almost a full year before the July 1999 late-night chat show appearance. The great Calista Conflagration began when The Actress turned up at the 1998 Emmys, looking very glamorous and Audrey Hepburn-like in that dress – a little sleeveless, scooped-back, nearly backless, pinkish-white Richard Tyler number – that emphasized how bone thin she was…

Why, she's as thin and bony as a new-born sparrow!

The immediate reaction to her couldn't have been more shocked if she'd stepped from her limousine wearing absolutely nothing at all.

Was she anorexic, bulimic, unbalanced or on drugs? Surely, no one could be that thin naturally! And it didn't help that her sensibility was so obviously brittle and she was more than a little thin-skinned on the subject of her weight.

'98 LBS!' the tabloid headlines screamed. 'ALLY ON A FAST-FOOD DIET!' And that was just the beginning.

Connie Chung is a spirited interviewer and an experienced TV newswoman, often underrated, who is married to tabloid-TV veteran Maury Povich, and she has known some tabloid and media attention of her own.

A couple of months before that remarkable July late-night appearance, at the height of all the intertwined controversies, it was she who snagged The Actress for an extensive and exclusive interview for 20/20, the ABC TV news-magazine hour. Providently, that interview aired at the very beginning of the May Sweeps, one of the three month-long periods so crucial to the television industry in the United States, when local viewing levels are extensively measured and the all-important advertising rates are set.

It was just at this very time, too, that the Great Anorexia Controversy intersected with the great debate over What Ally Meant For Feminism, and whether or not she was a fit heir to Mary Richards (Mary Tyler Moore), who was TV America's first spunky/nervous/cute (but rarely annoying) TV exemplar of young, single, professional womanhood. For Chung, getting that interview was seen at the time as quite a coup.

'Ally is a vulnerable loser when it comes to men,' the interviewer declared in soothing, almost hushed tones, typical of her voice-over remarks during the televised segment.

She was not Ally McBeal, The Actress averred to the TV interviewer, as if it was all just some simple mistake. They were seated across from each other, in matching straight-backed chairs that, except for a small, light-coloured wooden table and a vase of flowers, were the only decorations on a sparse, diffusely lighted set.

Forthrightly The Actress added that she did 'certainly have the tendency to take on the role that I'm playing'.

And Ally was just a character she played. Unlike Ally, she was not 'preoccupied' with finding a man. Nor did she 'sit back and wait for things to happen'.

The confusion between actress and character wasn't confined to one TV interlocutor or even to the tabloid press alone. *Time*, a popular weekly magazine, had put The Actress's face – but with the character's name – on a recent cover, along with such icons of the feminist movement as Susan B. Anthony, Betty Friedan and Gloria Steinem, and had pointedly asked, 'Is Feminism Dead?'

The portentous question had been posed in lettering arranged right above The Actress's head.

It was as if Ally McBeal, taking one pratfall too many, had killed the entire women's movement all by herself, and The Actress responded to the TV interviewer's obligatory feminism and biology-is-destiny questions with just a hint of annoyance.

Yes, she was a feminist. Certainly. She believed in equal opportunity and equal rights, too.

No, she didn't particularly listen to the ticking of the biological clock, nor was this even one of her big worries. The question itself couldn't help but remind a tabloid-savvy viewer that the TV interviewer herself had taken a break from her successful TV news career while she tried unsuccessfully to conceive a child.

On the subject of 'having it all', The Actress doubted it was possible…or even particularly desirable.

Then clever Connie Chung, no doubt looking to strike a few sparks, asked the young – and even younger looking – thirty-something woman her age.

'Are you thirty-four?' she asked directly. It was a question The Actress was famously averse to answering in public.

Her hazel eyes narrowed. A low, warning murmur, like a delicate growl, sounded in the back of her throat, not unlike Ling Woo's warning sound-effects growl on her show.

'Bad question,' she said tartly. 'I don't answer that question.'

The interviewer feigned surprise and, in a rush, The Actress, who after all was still new to the bear-baiting tricks of celebrity TV interviewers, explained her firm and sincere belief that asking a woman her age was something that, well, is simply not done.

'That's so old-fashioned!' the interviewer interjected, giving the quarry another quick poke.

'Maybe I'm an old-fashioned girl,' said The Actress quickly, reverting at once to a formula she'd used with snoopy interviewers before: 'As an actress, I want to remain a chameleon.'

Now that she had The Actress stirred up, the celebrity TV interviewer pounced, asking her the powder-keg question:

'Do you have an eating disorder?'

The Actress stared back at her with a sad-eyed frown of a smile – Et tu, Connie? – precisely the look moviegoers knew from so many Audrey Hepburn pictures, films like *Roman Holiday*, *The Nun's Story* and *Funny Face*. It was the reaction with which Hepburn, The Actress's elegant, gamine-faced doppelgänger, so eloquently registered her quiet disappointment – perhaps with an overly persistent suitor, but more likely with a heartless world.

'No,' The Actress replied finally. 'No.'

'What do you think I'm going to say,' she added, giving her intent interlocutor an actorly look of mock sincerity, '"Yeah, I do"? I would never say that in a million years.' She faltered ever so slightly, for the merest half-beat. 'This is the problem with this disease...People who have this disease are in denial.

'I cannot win in this situation.' She put her hands out from her sides in a silent plea. 'Which is what happened throughout this year...I was stuck between a rock and hard place. I don't have an eating disorder,' she said unequivocally, pointing out sensibly enough that if she had had one, under the pressure of the media spotlight, she would have 'gone down'.

But her dilemma was that the media commanded her to prove a negative. 'My only proof,' she said, 'is that, "Hello, I'm here".'

And then The Actress, arguably more feisty than wary, added the challenging remark that would soon be broadcast round the world. Eyeing the svelte, oh-so-concerned-looking interviewer appraisingly, she observed:

'I was thinking that you look very thin too.'

The TV interviewer, not only svelte but a tiny woman herself, smiled with ostensible sympathy and replied that, yes, in fact people regularly did tell her that she looked too thin, even unwell.

Above all, The Actress's instincts were to act, and she instantly put herself into the Connie Chung part of that imaginary conversation in which Chung had just been asked, 'Are you unwell?'

'Are you jealous?' The Actress-as-Chung said, giving the emotionally correct answer, the one that Connie Chung herself must have at the very least thought.

Then, reverting to her own persona, she turned right into the camera, looking it directly in the eye. 'Just thought I'd throw that catty remark in there,' she said jauntily, going on to point out that people wouldn't dare to come up to an overweight person and say, 'You're fat.' It was, after all, simply and self-evidently good manners, and good sense.

The entire brouhaha, she explained in conclusion, was over the fact that she'd lost a mere four pounds and that she looked much thinner on camera because she'd begun to work out.

She'd been studying kick-boxing, Hollywood's trendiest workout regimen du jour. And at that point in the *20/20* segment, as she spoke, footage was played of The Actress backstage at an awards show, the ropy muscles on her skeletally thin, bare upper arms flexing as she hoisted a statuette.

Given the highly charged circumstances, her answer was relatively complete and nicely nuanced and textured. Unfortunately, it was completely wrong for TV, which reflexively reduces titillating controversies like this one to shards and soundbites.

And the soundbite that resulted – 'I was thinking that you look very thin too...Are you jealous?' – that was played and replayed – seemed to show an obviously tense and hostile young woman, probably caught out in dire circumstances and denial, firing back defensively: 'You look very thin too.' The verdict, if only implicit: Guilty as charged.

Flash forward to July. After being announced once and cancelling at the very last minute (and annoying the boyish, gap-toothed host), The Actress, returning to the New York stage on her TV hiatus, finally came on that late-night TV talk show which originated from New York and was generally regarded as the hipper, if lower-rated, of the two that aired nightly at the same time. Also on the show that night was a late-night perennial, a folksy naturalist and zookeeper accompanied by a collection of cute exotic animals.

We've got a 'big big-time star' tonight, said the host, adding that she was currently also starring off-Broadway in a 'critically acclaimed, sold-out production'.

She entered the set to a wave of applause, striding in wearing a mannish outfit – black trousers and jacket over a light-blue shirt and white running shoes without socks. She shook hands firmly with the host who, towering over her, kissed her hand and led her to a chair.

'Welcome to the show,' he said in his uninflected Midwestern American accent, as she took a seat. Complimenting her on her outfit, he asked if after she was 'here' she had to run out and do her play.

'Thank you,' she replied. 'I do indeed.'

And as was the host's wont, he proceeded to enquire first about matters on the slightly absurd periphery, wanting to know the difference between a monologue and soliloquy. 'Are they the same thing essentially?' he asked deadpan.

'Yah,' she said, nodding her head up and down. Her honey-blonde hair fell to her shoulders and she held her hands together primly in her lap. Her legs were crossed tightly at the knees. She looked back at him directly, if warily, responding to his mock-serious silliness with a small smile on her face.

Had she memorized her thirty-five-minute monologue by rote, the host asked, was it in there, in her head, all computer-like?

'More human than computer-like, but yah' – she screwed her face up in a thoughtful frown – 'yah.'

'Do you ever go on autopilot,' the host continued wackily, 'where you're thinking about, you know, "Hmm, those frozen waffles are damn good"?'

Her head bobbed up and down in agreement. 'It's amazing how you can be thinking one thing and saying another,' she said genially, and it was easy for the viewer to wonder if, even then, right at that second, she was thinking, 'Aha, here it comes: the subject of food!'

In any case, they carried on, the host wondering if the audience for her play could tell when her attention was elsewhere. It was hard to know with 'this audience', she replied, once again taking the question at face value. 'It's certainly not a comfortable night in the theatre.'

'No Neil Simon,' the host interjected, 'no Whoop-De-Doo Boys or whatever it is.'

The audience laughed and The Actress chuckled along, a warm and girlish sound, as she fidgeted slightly, kicking her crossed leg up and down.

'Now what happened, you were supposed to be here a couple months ago?' the host asked, shifting gears abruptly on the laugh – something he was practised at doing; he'd done it to Cher, to Madonna and a hundred other lesser, and less controversial, celebrity lights. The Actress, her legs curled tightly together, hands seemingly jammed in her lap, scrunched ever tighter into her seat.

'I went nuts,' the host continued with a dryness that could be mistaken for merriment, 'I went crazy when I heard you cancelled because' – and here came the punchline – 'when we get a big star, often they don't come back.'

The audience laughed uproariously. The Actress giggled along, seeming to relax a bit. 'And I was nervous, you know. So I was ready to go crazy on you, because at the last minute your plans changed and I took it personally, I was insulted, and I was this close' – the host held thumb and forefinger together in front of The Actress's face.

There was a big laugh and they went on to talk about the Dancing Baby from the TV show. The host had a graphic ready to roll and out came a reasonable representation of Ally's very own Dancing Baby, boogying across the screen.

Watching it on a monitor off to the side, The Actress laughed too. 'Kick it!' she said gaily, aiming a kick at the computer-generated image (but apparently because her view in the monitor was reversed, the running shoe she aimed went off towards the wrong side of the screen). She turned back to the host, a smile on her face, brushing a strand of hair away from her face.

'And I identify the Dancing Baby as the single creepiest thing on television,' the host observed quite sensibly.

'Aah,' The Actress said, nodding up and down in general agreement. She 'didn't mind' it so much on television, she said, but when they were shooting it there was a 'baby on a stick'.

The host fairly pounced on the line. 'That's illegal,' he said, stabbing a finger out for emphasis, a goofy smile on his rubbery face. 'I'm no child-care expert, but…'

Again the audience screamed with delight, and into the laughter the host dispatched his very own version of the Dancing Baby – a fat man in a nappy dancing to a chorus of BOOM-ACHUCKA-BOOM-ACHUCKA.

The Actress gasped in mock amazement, and smiled broadly, though the amusement never reached her eyes, while the audience hooted and clapped, and the host just grinned his daffy, crooked grin.

The Actress looked down, as if embarrassed. 'He has a wife and kids,' the host said with a smile. And then they went to a commercial.

And when they came back from the break, with only a brief preamble about the zookeeper backstage and his monkey full of Nyquil, a patent cold medicine, he asked the inevitable question: 'Now how come everybody was goin' nuts about your weight and that sort of thing, and it's been goin' on forever? You must be sick of that.'

As he spoke, she tilted her head to one side, looking up at him through momentarily lowered eyes.

'You can't win,' he observed, then asked, 'Are you comfortable with the weight you're at?'

'I am,' she said brightly, as the camera cut to the inevitable close shot of her face. 'I feel good.'

'Is it over?'

'You know, I don't really know,' she said, rocking a bit in her chair, 'I don't really pay attention any more. I'm very, very bored with the whole thing. It's boring.'

'Good for you,' said the host, seeming for once to mean it.

The Actress looked down, putting a forefinger to her lip, as if pondering seriously. She looked up, eyebrows arched, a pixyish smile lighting up her pixyish face.

She looked down, then glanced sideways at the host. 'I would like to take this opportunity just to tell the press,' she began sweetly enough on that late-night, nationally broadcast TV show.

Then, hazel eyes flashing, she turned full-face into the camera and with a drop-dead smoulder in those big eyes, she exclaimed: 'KISS MY SKINNY WHITE ASS!'

The audience dissolved in laughter and applause.

Calista Flockhart – The Vital (and Not So Vital) Statistics

BIRTHPLACE:

Freeport, Illinois.

DATE OF BIRTH:

Most likely 11 November 1964.

AGE:

Thirtysomething. Understandably, given Hollywood's penchant for nymphets and the perpetual lack of good roles for all other women, she simply refuses to say more. Reports put her age in mid-1999 at thirty-four.

MOTHER:

Kay, a high-school English teacher, now retired.

FATHER:

Ronald, a Kraft Foods quality-control executive, now retired, whose work required him to move his young family around the American Middle West – from Illinois to Iowa to Minnesota – and then on to New Jersey.

BROTHER:

Gary (older).

HER BROTHER'S CHILDHOOD NICKNAME FOR HER:

Pumpkin Head – because her head was always too big for her body. Interestingly enough, some analysts of the actors who achieve long-lasting success on series television believe that along with talent, connections and luck, it's better to have a head that's large in proportion to the torso. Why ever would that be? It's because the camera 'likes' that proportion better.

WHERE SHE SPENT HER CHILDHOOD SUMMERS:

In Boone, Iowa, a town named after frontiersman Daniel Boone, where her grandparents lived. She summered there from around the age of five until she was in her twenties.

HOW SHE THOUGHT OF HERSELF AS A CHILD:

Improbably enough, she thought of herself as the 'strong, silent type – and maybe the comedian'. As she told one reporter (*New York Times*, 2 May 1999), 'I spent a lot of time alone, fantasizing. Some people kind of live in their minds and some people socialize. I was sort of a person who did both.'

HER JUNIOR HIGH SCHOOL BAND INSTRUMENT:

Flute.

Though it's probably not appropriate to put too much emphasis on the generalization, this is certainly one of those instruments that, partly because it requires breath control to master, tends to attract students who are more self-controlled, perhaps even more tightly wound than their class-mates.

EDUCATION:

Shawnee High School, Medford, New Jersey, where she was a junior varsity cheerleader and a member of the student council.

Rutgers University: a 1987 graduate, with a degree in theatre.

FIRST PROFESSIONAL STAGE APPEARANCE:

In the drama *Beside Herself*, playing opposite film actor William Hurt.

FIRST CAREER BREAK:

That came in 1994, on the New York stage, in a revival of Tennessee Williams' *The Glass Menagerie*, playing Laura Wingfield, the shy girl at the emotional centre of this much-lauded story, an American classic. It's a notoriously difficult role for any actress (Laura, crippled and vulnerable, a collector of delicate glass figurines, can easily be made to seem simply pitiful or to become tedious), but Calista won rave, career-making reviews, such as the one in a national magazine that declared her interpretation of the excruciatingly shy Laura to be 'near perfect'.

THE OTHER ROLES:

Even actors who are seemingly sudden, overnight, incandescent successes rarely go directly from the mythical apothecary soda fountain right to the Hollywood sound stage. On the surface, Calista Flockhart may have seemed to come from out of nowhere to a kind of universal celebrity, but before Ally she was a hard-working young actress, remarkably well thought of on the New York stage, and taking the kind of small commercial roles that were often beneath critical notice. First among them was the part of Elise in 1989 on the long-running daytime television soap opera *The Guiding Light*.

Then came a role in *Darrow*, a 1991 TV movie, and in 1994 the part of the unnamed Barnard Girl in *Quiz Show*, Robert Redford's dissection of the American TV quiz-show scandals of the late fifties. Calista was also in such small pictures as *Getting In* and *Naked in New York*, both in 1994, and played the title role in a 1996 movie called *Pictures of Baby Jane Doe*. That film was never released in cinemas, but went straight to video.

SECOND CAREER BREAK:

That came in 1996, when director Mike Nichols cast her in *The Birdcage*, the American remake of *La Cage Aux Folles*. As the timid fiancée, her role was small but pivotal, while the rest of the cast, which included Robin Williams, Nathan Lane and Gene Hackman as her father, a right-wing United States senator, was high-powered and high-profile. Still, she was widely and favourably noticed, by Hollywood and film critics alike.

THIRD CAREER BREAK:

That came in 1997, on the New York stage, in the Roundabout Theater Company's production of Chekhov's *The Three Sisters*, playing Natasha, Andrei's manipulative wife, alongside Amy Irving, Lili Taylor and Jeanne Tripplehorn.

FOURTH CAREER BREAK:

While still on stage in the Chekhov, she was called out to Los Angeles to audition for a new television series. She was ambivalent at best, as she's recalled it, putting the whole idea up for discussion by her fellow *Sisters* actors, who urged her to go. So on a Sunday evening, after the house lights dimmed at that night's stage performance, she boarded an overnight flight to LA for her Monday morning audition before a small group of producers and executives. Of course, she thought she'd failed.

But writer–producer David E. Kelley, after auditioning the proverbial thousands and thousands of young hopefuls, cast the New York stage actress who'd made her mark playing shy or shy-and-neurotic characters, as Ally McBeal.

Calista closed down her lower Manhattan apartment and headed West.

CONSTANT COMPANION:

Though she's been linked romantically by the press with actor Ben Stiller and others, including two of the producers of her own TV show, her constant companion, the one with whom she moved from New York to an apartment in West Hollywood, is actually an eight-year-old terrier named Webster.

CURRENT HOME:

West Los Angeles

DRESS SIZE:

Two. Or is it Zero?

THE USUAL DISGUISE:

For going out in public unnoticed, it's a baseball cap and oversized sunglasses.

HER FAVOURITE STORE:

The Gap, near Rodeo Drive, in Beverly Hills.

HER FAVOURITE SWEATER COLOUR:

Grey.

HER FAVOURITE SWEATER:

A grey Sears sweater that once belonged to her grandfather.

HER FAVOURITE PJS:

White, draw-string pyjamas.

WHAT SHE EATS FOR BREAKFAST:

Spinach, or so the press reported, occasioning much hilarity.

WHAT SHE EATS FOR LUNCH, TAKE ONE:

That's closely scrutinized by the press as well, so when she met an interviewer and opted to order a cappuccino and a tall orange juice for her entire meal, it was duly chewed over for its larger implications.

WHAT SHE EATS FOR LUNCH, TAKE TWO:

Stopping with another journalist at a coffee shop, she ordered a salad and a turkey sandwich. Whether or not she cleaned her plate was not reported.

WHAT SHE EATS FOR LUNCH, TAKE THREE:

You'd think she'd learn not to keep having these lunch-hour interviews, but in Hollywood feeding the press while meeting the press is a local tradition, and so she met yet another journalist, this time at the luxury Hotel Bel-Air, dining on a 'large' chicken sandwich and two skimmed milk cappuccinos.

WHAT SHE EATS FOR LUNCH, TAKE FOUR:

Another reporter, another duly memorialized lunch, this time at a West Hollywood restaurant. After noting that Calista had finished off a spinach, tomato and cheese egg-white omelette, the journalist posed the obligatory question: Had she truly been that hungry or was she just 'playing healthy for a reporter'?

DINNER:

Promoting a movie (in this case, *A Midsummer Night's Dream*) means meeting the press *ad nauseam*, and sometimes that even means eating dinner twice, once on the set and once more, along with a Los Angeles magazine writer, in a trendy West Hollywood restaurant. There she dined on a 'healthful' seaweed salad and grilled ahi tuna with black pepper sauce, bread and butter, all washed down with a glass of Merlot. And yes, she did 'empty' her plate.

WHAT SHE SAYS SHE DOES IN HER SPARE TIME:

Decorates her new house...Takes kick-boxing lessons...Drinks camomile tea and reads a good book...

WHAT HER CO-STARS AND COLLEAGUES SAY:

'She's very strong-willed...I don't know anyone who has had a successful career in show business that you could describe as "fragile".' – Greg Germann (Richard Fish on *Ally*), *TV Guide*, 1 May 1999.

'All stars fit some archetype...[and] people are drawn to Calista as an archetype of the Little Match Girl – this very sensitive waif who at the same time houses a remarkable strength.' – Michael Hoffman (director of *A Midsummer Night's Dream*), *In Style*, May 1999.

'Compared to Calista, everyone seems big.' – Jane Krakowski (Elaine Vassal on *Ally*), *TV Guide*, 26 September 1998.

WHAT 'CALISTA' MEANS:

'Most beautiful.' From the Greek. One of its many variants is 'Calisto', which is also the name given to a large satellite of the planet Jupiter, and was, according to Greek mythology, a nymph. Calisto was loved by Zeus, then changed into a she-bear by the jealous Hera and later became the constellation Ursa Major, or the Great Bear.

WHAT CALISTA MEANS:

Sometimes Hollywood seems absolutely filled with excruciatingly thin women, anorexic or bulimic or just doing coke or speed, who either aspire to be or perhaps even actually are on TV. Anyone with more than a passing acquaintance with the business could name you famous names. But just because somebody whispers it, or even shouts it, about one particular actress doesn't mean it's true.

Take Calista Flockhart: She says she can't win and it's true. She is so direct and challenging when asked intrusive questions, yet she must know that talking back to the press is just taken as more evidence that she's unbalanced. As she told *In Style* magazine

(May 1999): 'If somebody tells me not to do something, I'll do it faster, louder and bigger than ever.'

Thin? Yes. Naturally so? Hey, it's possible. Sick? Doubtful.

She seems uncommonly convincing when she insists (as she did in May 1999, in *George* magazine) that 'just because you're thin, [it] doesn't mean you're diseased. If you're thin, and you're healthy, there are certain people in the world who are going to be pissed off about it. It's discrimination.'

Discrimination?

'If I had big boobs, none of this would have happened.'

'I don't believe my weight is a problem,' she said in *TV Guide* around the same time. It's a point she'd made before, over and over again: 'It's society's obsession with my weight that's the problem.'

HER AGENT:

Bill Butler at the Gersh Agency.

The Jokes

One is tempted to say she made a fat target, certainly an easy one for stand-up comics and late-night monologists alike. Someone with a cynical cast of mind, a Hollywood insider perhaps, might even be tempted to wonder how much of the tempest was concocted with forethought; after all, it was a windfall of (free) publicity, of which it is said there's no such thing as bad – and her publicists are the best.

Some were funny, some were cruel, but in 1998 and 1999 Calista jokes like these were all the rage:

'Stop comparing me to Kate Moss!' a comic says indignantly, reading a letter allegedly written by Calista Flockhart. 'I'm nothing like that fat pig.'

In the first two minutes of the first episode of *Movie Stars*, a new situation comedy about married movie stars living in Malibu, California, a delivery man brings a deluxe wicker basket of muffins to the door. The attached note, ostensibly an apology for a missed appointment, reads: 'Sorry…I got hungry. Love, Calista Flockhart.'

In a late-night sketch-comedy parody on the long-running *Saturday Night Live*, 'Sean Connery', 'Nicholas Cage' and 'Calista Flockhart' are playing the celebrity version of *Jeopardy*, a well-known and long-running TV game show. All three 'celebrities' are played for laughs as unspeakably arrogant and dumb, and 'Calista' is portrayed as a slack-faced, stringy-haired dimwit whose wrong answers have earned a 'negative $58,000' total. She doesn't write any answer at all to the final question ('The category is horsies: Are horsies pretty? We'll accept either answer') because the 'pen is too heavy.'

Naturally both the other celebrities get the answer wrong too.

VH–1, which stands for 'Video Hits', is a 24-hour cable music channel, on the model of (and owned by the same corporation as) MTV. Like its sister channel, VH–1 has recently got into the business of made-for-TV award shows.

That in itself is ripe for satire. And so, inevitably, the practice of portentous but meaningless award shows, which allow the stars yet another televised moment of sanctimoniousness and press puffery, got the treatment on another *Saturday Night Live* sketch.

It's the first annual 'VH–1 Spirituality Awards'... An actor portraying a fey host introduces an actor playing Will Smith and an actress playing Madonna, dressed in a sari, who receives the Mahatma Gandhi Award and prattles on about the rigours of her 'ten-week spiritual journey'. Then out come the next two presenters – Calista Flockhart and...Christ!

Like presenters at all televised award shows they have the obligatory teleprompter banter to get through, so of course Christ has to rather sheepishly put on his eye glasses, the better to read the canned dialogue:

'Gee, Calista,' he 'reads' in the familiar stilted and flat intonation of the under-rehearsed celebrity, 'you look really skinny. You should try my loaves-and-fishes diet.'

'Let's do lunch,' says Calista, 'my people will call your people.'

Better hurry up and get started then, Christ replies, because I've got millions and millions of people. And as the two actors shuffle off the stage, the fey host gives them a look, then delivers the punchline: 'He's a carpenter,' he says heartily, 'and she looks like Karen Carpenter.'

And so it went on and on until the odds of an improbable event happening were said to be 'even slimmer than Ally McBeal'.

The Feminist Cultural Critic

Camille Paglia, author of *Sexual Personae* and other works, an essayist and feminist intellectual known for her sharp critiques of popular culture, was unsparing when it came to Calista Flockhart. 'She looks diseased,' Paglia told the *Los Angeles Times* (20 June 1999). 'She keeps on carrying on about how "I'm fine" and "I have no eating disorder", but it is a disorder if you're that thin and you choose a dress that is backless.'

Excerpt From an Irate Letter...

To the Editor, from a reader of the *Los Angeles Times*, 27 June 1999:

'Why is it so hard for people to understand that thin people are that way because it's simply in their genes to be skinny? As a 5-foot-7, 115-pound female, I can vouch for Calista. It is possible to eat whatever you want and not gain any weight. There is such a thing as moderation and a junk food-free diet.'

Pay No Attention to the Woman Behind the Curtain...

*Yes there is a real Wizard of Oz behind
the glamorous tinsel curtain.*

Her name is Pat Kingsley and she has changed the way the Hollywood entertainment-publicity business works. It's hard to overstate her importance.

If you've ever watched a red-carpet celebrity promenade before a premiere, a charity gala or a glittering award show, you've seen her – she's the tall, rather severe- and alert-looking blonde woman at the star's elbow, the one hovering in the immediate background while Tom or Nicole or Jodie or Courtney or Arnold or some other A-list luminary-of-the-day is being interviewed and delivering the soundbite you will see on the news.

Kingsley, most often described as acerbic, tight-lipped or intimidating, is one of the founding partners of PMK, a public relations company formed in 1980, which was recently acquired by the McCann-Erickson advertising agency, a unit of the Interpublic Group. Other PMK clients include Woody Allen, Mariah Carey, Matt Damon, Johnny Depp, Tom Hanks, Dustin Hoffman, Lisa Kudrow, Jennifer Lopez, Michelle Pfeiffer, Robert Redford and Meryl Streep.

For most of its existence PMK has been generally regarded as the most powerful press agency in Hollywood. It's known not only as the premiere 'praisery', as *Variety* calls PR agencies, with the most high-powered roster of celebrity clients, but it's also the one the stars turn to when they want to manage publicity, rather than simply attract the glare of the spotlight; in other words, to say no. For example, in 1989, when the press learned that Rob Lowe, a teen favourite, had videotaped himself having three-way sex with a sixteen-year-old girl he'd picked up the year before in an Atlanta club, the actor turned to PMK to manage the media furore, and it was PMK who kept him away from reporters until the brouhaha subsided.

Even before that, probably beginning earlier in the 1980s with actress Jodie Foster, who since the John Hinckley affair had had her own reasons to be wary of the press, Kingsley had introduced the practice – now widespread – of demanding certain preconditions before turning her client over to an interviewer.

Kingsley demanded – and got – the promise of a publication's cover before agreeing to co-operate with a story about a client. Kingsley demanded – and got – the photographer of her choice and a veto over the images that could be printed. Kingsley even demanded – and got – veto power over which writer an editor could assign.

To her credit, she pushed the envelope of the acceptable in the interest of her clients, and the famous and powerful flocked to her because of it. She was the first to make profitable use of a hard economic fact: in a starstruck time like ours, a magazine that could tout an 'exclusive' interview with Tom Cruise – and that could put his boyish visage on the cover – would see its sales soar. To their discredit, editors and journalists alike, whether print or TV, caved in to her demands in droves, giving up their traditional independence and control for the short-term revenue or ratings advantage of PMK's beneficence.

Not surprisingly, the result was that the most starstruck writers and reporters, the very individuals who could be reliably counted on to avoid tough questions and sensitive issues, were the ones who got the go-ahead from PMK. Others, including some of the most prominent in America, were cast out from PMK's charmed circle. In Hollywood, the method Kingsley and PMK pioneered is now commonplace.

Which brings us back to The Actress. In the late spring and early summer of 1999, at a time when she had a theatrical motion picture to promote (*A Midsummer Night's Dream*, the latest updating of a project penned originally by the hottest British writer in Hollywood since Jane Austen), Calista Flockhart did a number of magazine interviews, and lo and behold, she turned up on cover after cover – *George*, *In Style*, *Los Angeles* and *TV Guide* among them. She also did TV interviews, including the morning news and talk shows.

Of all the American morning chat shows, the most senior, the one where the morning talk-show format was invented, is called *Today*. It's broadcast by the NBC Network, and it is one of the traditional three morning-TV stops for celebrities, politicos, authors and passing 'newsmakers' exploiting their allotted fifteen minutes of fame.

In the spring of 1999, PMK once again drew the line: Calista would not go on the *Today* show to discuss why she was so thin; questions about the subject were forbidden. *Today*, refusing to play along, summarily cancelled the scheduled interview.

In the wake of the cancellation in April 1999, Kingsley was candid about her method. 'Yes, we try to control,' she told the *New York Times*. 'We try to control whether or not it's a cover. We cop to that. We ask who the writer is. If it's somebody that either we or the client has had a bad experience with, we say, well, that's not going to work. They either will come back with another writer or won't do the story.'

But the agency, with its stellar roster of clients, had another recourse beyond simply saying no and killing the interview or the story, and it was one that Hollywood understood well: exacting revenge.

One of the most hotly anticipated films in years was *Eyes Wide Shut* starring Tom Cruise and Nicole Kidman. It was director

Stanley Kubrick's final film, and the picture's July press junket was the hot summer ticket.

A junket brings together movie reviewers and writers from all around the country, usually in Los Angeles or New York, and they are wined, dined, shown a preview of an upcoming film and are allowed to interview its stars, usually in a group setting. Until recent years, studios paid all the expenses for such trips; now, many of the larger and more reputable publications pay travel and hotel expenses for their entertainment writers.

But PMK, representing Cruise, circulated a waiver at the junket that, when signed, gave it the right to see rough cuts of any TV features and, more importantly, to veto footage prior to broadcast. The waiver also included language binding the journalists to 'not show the artist [i.e. Cruise] in a negative or derogatory manner', according to the *Los Angeles Times*. The rough-cut provision was a mistake that was deleted from the waiver, but it still retained the no-derogatory-story language, Kingsley told the *Times*.

In the wake of that controversial junket Cruise and Kidman turned up on the morning talk shows to promote their film. Cruise appeared on ABC's *Good Morning America*, while the third-rated morning show, CBS's *This Morning*, had Kidman. For NBC's *Today*, there was nothing.

According to the *New York Post*, 'media insiders say NBC was left out in the cold because *Today* producers refused in April to promise that [interviewer] Matt Lauer would avoid asking Flockhart, who denies she's anorexic, about her weight. When NBC balked at Kingsley's demand, PMK cancelled Flockhart's appearance...Payback time came when the Cruise interview was up for grabs.'

Predictably, a PMK spokesperson denied the *Post* report, saying, 'There is no connection.'

The Ally Factor in US Politics

The Actress was peeved by the controversy over her weight, quite plainly so, and maybe a considerable bit more, but as a new millennium approached she wasn't the only thin single woman who was annoyed. Millions of young, urban, single professional women without children were fuming too. For years pontificating politicians, professing to be knightly champions of traditional values, had vowed to fight for the Traditional Family and had offered succour to harried Soccer Moms. Standing up for what was called Mom and Apple Pie was the way to get elected. Everyone knew that, just as everyone knew that, somehow, unmarried women didn't count.

Then along came *The Rules* and *Bridget Jones's Diary*, and a cultural flowering called Girl Power. Somewhere in America, a policy wonk poring over the dry details of past election results realized that in the 1996 election, nearly a full three-quarters (73%, to be precise) of all young, urban, single women without children living in the north-eastern United States had voted for William Jefferson Clinton as President, and it was they – not the celebrated Soccer Moms of the south and south-western suburbs – who'd made the difference. In fact, in the 2000 election it would be they who would hold the balance of power.

'Clinton seduced me, I like to say,' one of these young women – thin, long-haired, attractive and obviously highly-strung – told an interviewer with a shrug. And so it was that in the last year of the twentieth century, as the race for President of the United States lumbered into high gear amidst the usual hoopla, American politicians of every stripe began to reconsider their electoral strategy. Their worried advisers huddled, strategizing late into the night. They gave their disquiet a name, the only one possible:

They called it the Ally Demographic and brainstormed, devising scenarios to cope with the 'Ally Gap'.

In Hollywood, surely, a certain prolific television writer–producer was amused.

Nighty Night

How do you measure the larger influence of a fictional TV show? Its presence in the political discourse of a great nation is one way. Another is by the grist it offers for comedians and jokes. Yet another, of course, is by the merchandising opportunities it spins off.

Everyone knows Ally McBeal has an active dream life and that after a tiring day at the law office, she can often be found padding around the flat she shares with Renee (Lisa Nicole Carson) in an oversize pair of sky blue pyjamas decorated with fluffy white sheep. Now fans of the show can snuggle up in front of the television in their very own official Ally McBeal pyjamas, as well as what is called 'lounge wear', all of it decorated with such snappy remarks from the show as…'snappish'. Also on the way to a shop near you: a line of Ally workout wear.

To sleep, perchance to dream? Aye, there's the kick.

The Kernel –
How Ally Was Conceived

Way back in the mid-1980s, or so the story goes, the president of NBC Entertainment wanted to create a new show that would both reflect the spirits of the times and appeal to teenage boys. Meeting two producers for lunch, he had a brainwave. The network president pulled out a pen and scribbled something on a napkin, which he passed over to the producers. On it they read the words MTV Cops, and from that kernel came the series *Miami Vice*.

Almost a decade and a half later, the president of Fox Broadcasting wanted a new show to follow *Melrose Place* and go on opposite ABC's *Monday Night Football*, the venerable sports programme that attracts a mostly male audience. He turned to the prolific writer–producer David E. Kelley, who had also created *Picket Fences*, *The Practice* and *Chicago Hope*. What the network president said to the prolific producer was, 'Go and create a series with a strong female lead, one who appeals to women, ages eighteen to thirty-four.'

Why?

She didn't want to do it originally, she has said that repeatedly, she didn't want to go to Hollywood to do TV, she wanted to stay on the New York stage. But…

'I was really tired of being poor. It's very difficult to make a living in the theater, and I was so sick to death of living hand to mouth. I thought, What do you have to lose?' (*Los Angeles*, June 1999).

How the Critics Greeted the Debut of the Show in 1997

They were smitten. Mostly.

'It is happiness indeed to start off the new season with a show worth loving,' crooned *TV Guide* (20 September 1997). '*Ally McBeal* – and the woman it's about – is everything that I want in a series (and that any man would want in a woman): smart, fresh, funny, warm, wry, and well-produced.'

That wasn't the way the influential *Los Angeles Times* (8 September 1997) saw it, grousing that the show 'has nothing between the ears and is notable largely for boobs and Barbies – walking shampoo commercials with masses of glistening long hair and long legs in short skirts tailored to babe-watching.' But in the first critical chorus that was the minority opinion.

'David E. Kelley adds another jewel to his telecrown,' rhapsodized the *Hollywood Reporter* (8 September 1997), cautioning nonetheless that the story of a young Harvard Law grad starting out at the same Boston law firm that employs the one-time love of her life, Billy Alan Thomas (Gil Bellows), and his wife, Georgia Thomas (Courtney Thorne-Smith), was a 'meager premise' and 'thin fantasy material that often stumbles over the line of cute'.

'Female viewers are fascinated and male viewers seem mesmerized – making *Ally McBeal* this season's word-of-mouth hit,' enthused the *Orange County Register* (19 October 1997), another Southern California newspaper. It wondered, however: 'Will Kelley allow Ally to steady herself, to go mature? If not, she could become a boring doormat.'

And from *Daily Variety* (8 September 1997) came: 'Offbeat, engaging and smartly written – and with a can't-miss lead in Broadway actress Calista Flockhart…Only the talented [David E.] Kelley…could make insufferable yuppies this much fun.'

The David E. Kelley Factor on US TV

Apparently when you're a writer–producer prince, you rule absolutely and can get away with almost anything, even in the ultra-competitive world of US television.

Which even means starting a two-part episode of one of your shows on one network, and finishing it on another one of your series, on a competing network.

Still it's incredible that TV's premier writer–producer, the almost unbelievably productive David E. Kelley, got away with a two-hour story that intermixed the casts of his *Ally McBeal* and *The Practice*.

Ally is on Fox and *The Practice* is on ABC, two networks whose member stations compete tooth and nail for viewers and advertising dollars. Both series are creations of the talented and prolific Mr Kelley, whose third well-regarded network series, *Chicago Hope*, is on yet another network, CBS.

The through-line story of the two-part 'Axe Murderer', which begins on *McBeal*, is about a Cage/Fish client accused of the axe murder of her husband; because they like their law 'soft-core', as Ally puts it, Ally's cagey legal fishers turn to Bobby (Dylan McDermott) and his *Practice* colleagues. Sure, they're both David Kelley series set in the world of Boston law, but the in-it-for-the-money brahmins of Cage/Fish and the hard-working lawyers with social consciences on *The Practice* are like vichyssoise and chowder.

'This place is a little too eccentric,' *The Practice*'s Bobby remarks, looking around at the denizens of Cage/Fish. 'You people are loose cannons…You're all crazy.'

The two-part episode also highlighted the sexual dichotomy between the two shows: with the exception of Cage and Fish, the two principals, and Billy, the unrequited love interest, the *Ally* 'loose cannons' are women; on *The Practice*, where they handle the tough cases, the focus is more often on the men.

Still, if Fox's viewers wanted to see how the *Ally* story turned out, they had to switch over to ABC, the competition, which cost the affiliated Fox stations dearly in American advertising dollars.

But then Mr Kelley is apparently worth it. ABC gave him an on-air commitment for *Snoops*, a new series set in the world of private investigators, which he will not write, only oversee, although he did pen the pilot himself. But it's not as if he doesn't have enough to do already.

He does write all of *Ally* and *The Practice*, quite a stunning output of clever and entertaining words in and of itself. And when his third series, *Chicago Hope* – a medical drama highly regarded by the critics, but never a smash in the ratings – from which he'd withdrawn his day-to-day oversight, was in danger of imminent cancellation, all it took was a promise from Kelley to turn his attention back to it, writing the 1999 season finale and the 2000 opener, to keep it on the air.

Kelley made that commitment partly because, as he told the television writer for the *New York Times* (28 July 1999), he believed he had 'given up too easily' when CBS cancelled an earlier, critically-acclaimed-but-low-rated series, his *Picket Fences*.

For his end-of-the-season attention-grabbing ploy, Kelley brought back popular stage-musical and theatrical-feature actor Mandy Patinkin in his Emmy Award-winning role as Dr Jeffrey Geiger, put him in charge of the hospital and had him fire almost every cast member who had been added to the production since Kelley left the show.

That included jettisoning Peter Berg, Jayne Brook, Vondie Curtis-Hall, Stacy Edwards, Christine Lahti and Eric Stoltz. Said Hector Elizondo, who survived the purge, many members of the cast and crew were 'in a state of shock, to put it mildly'.

Patinkin agreed to come back for at least seven of the thirteen new episodes that the network reportedly ordered on the basis of the Kelley Factor.

The Early Days of
David E. Kelley

Hip, *Law*, *Fences*, *Howser*, movie-star matrimony…those are some of the stepping stones in the early and apparently enviable progression of the young man named David E. Kelley, who graduated from Princeton in 1979.

In the mid-1980s he was just a recent graduate of Boston University Law School (1983) practising his profession, who'd discovered his flair for writing relatively late, always said he never had an ambition to write professionally and – just for the fun of it – had penned a story about a young lawyer.

That story was subsequently made into a movie (*From the Hip*, starring Judd Nelson and directed by Bob Clark, probably best known for directing *Porky's*).

Hip was widely thought of as a spoof of *LA Law*, the much-lauded eighties series from producer Stephen Bochco, who has created or co-created some of the most influential series in modern TV history, among them *Hill Street Blues* and *NYPD Blue*.

That was in itself mildly ironic, because it was that original story that first caught the attention of veteran writer–producer Bochco, who even then was staffing up his new series, *LA Law*, set in an upscale law firm in an upscale, high-rise west Los Angeles enclave called Century City (which, incidentally, was built on the onetime backlot of the nearby Twentieth Century Fox studio – hence the name – which also produces many of the Bochco shows and owns a network which just happens to air *Ally McBeal*).

In the time-honoured fashion Bochco brought the young lawyer with the literary flair west, to Los Angeles, to write an episode of the new show. The one episode turned to two, the two to three. Eventually the young writer was made story editor, and the show became a reliable awards magnet. When he left *Law* in the early nineties, he was its executive producer and the co-creator, with Bochco, of *Doogie Howser, MD*, a half-hour comedy about a teenage prodigy who becomes a medical doctor.

Success for the legally trained Hollywood writer who had never taken a writing class in university meant the unparalleled showbiz opportunity to create his own series, and what he came up with for the 1992 season was called *Picket Fences*. It was a series that never found its audience but was extremely well received by the critics from the very beginning.

Fences was avowedly influenced by *Northern Exposure*, a one-hour series that brought a new style of magical realism to primetime television, mixing light comedy with believable drama, as well as ever-increasing infusions of the wholly fanciful – pixie dust mixed with the uncanny. *Exposure* had Cicely, a picturesque hamlet on the erstwhile Alaskan Riviera; *Fences* had Rome, a picturesque hamlet somewhere in the vicinity of the Wisconsin Dells.

So, like *Northern Exposure*, which readily resorted to midget-sized green demons, spirits and hundred-year-old characters who turned up to narrate flashback episodes, in *Fences*, ostensibly a family drama about a small-town sheriff (Tom Skerritt), his doctor wife (Kathy Baker) and their children, you just might find an apparent murdered man in a Tin Man suit (from *The Wizard of Oz*), an apparent suicide in a dishwashing machine, a singing nun, a few hookers, a joke or two about the US Supreme Court and an apparent case of spontaneous human combustion.

By then, press reports were already duly noting that the movie actors in the show's cast had been lured to the TV project by the high quality of Kelley's writing. Right up to the CBS renewal of *Chicago Hope*, just because Kelley was back and composing, that's remained a theme. It would be tempting to dismiss it as simply clever press agentry, if not for one indisputable fact: the writing was very good, uncommonly so considering the prodigious output that was Kelley's other consistent hallmark. It was writing distinguished by a fine feeling for life's coincidences and absurdities and for the nuanced greys of character, so often rendered by TV in cheap and dramatically easy black-and-white.

As *Fences* went into the November Sweeps of its second, critically successful year, its creator was in Santa Barbara, California, about ninety minutes' drive north of Los Angeles, getting married in the charming old California seacoast town that had been the site of the 'Western White House' during the Reagan era.

His bride was film actress Michelle Pfeiffer, who'd been receiving adoring reviews in films like *The Age of Innocence*, *The Fabulous Baker Boys* and *Batman Returns*, a special-effects spectacle in which she stole the show with a captivating, bravura turn as the to-die-for-sexy Catwoman.

In an era of tabloid television and helicoptering paparazzi with telephoto lenses, this was one of the few weddings to take place outside the gaze of prying eyes. That's probably because bride and groom were wised up enough to keep the guest list small, and hold the ceremony under a white canopy in the lush grounds of a Mediterranean-style private home – far from the hot lights of Los Angeles and surrounded by a squad of edgy hired security. But, most of all, it was because they opted not to tell the guests in advance the exact nature of the ceremony they were attending.

A few months before, Pfeiffer, who was divorced from TV actor Peter Horton (*Thirtysomething*) after nine years of marriage, had adopted a child, and the approximately seventy assembled guests thought they'd been invited to the little eight-month-old girl's christening, which was in fact held right after the couple's wedding.

The ploy – clever, whimsical, romantic and just a touch mischievous – would not have been out of place in a David E. Kelley series, especially the one he would create a few years later.

A few weeks after the wedding, Pfeiffer guest starred as the voice of Mindy Simmons on the 'Last Temptation of Homer' episode of *The Simpsons*, the long-running animated series for adults, playing a beautiful co-worker at the Springfield nuclear power plant, who shares with the hapless Homer a weakness for donuts and nearly tempts him to adultery. Not surprisingly, she also guest starred in an episode of *Picket Fences*.

The Feedback Loop

The best writers on television, especially of hit multi-character ensemble shows with complex, interweaving plots, understand that today viewer and fan interest in the show extends to the real lives of the actors and actresses who play the characters.

People read the columns and the tabloids and watch the entertainment shows and tabloid TV. So the writers integrate not only the talents of their stars into the characters, but their foibles and escapades and controversies into the stories as well. No one does this better than David Kelley on *Ally McBeal*. For example:

Jane Krakowski is a former Broadway dancer, so naturally Elaine Vassal is often out on the dance floor too, once even partnering Ling Woo in a sexy swing competition. After Kelley spotted Jane fashionably smoking a stogy on set, Elaine developed a taste for cigars too.

No sooner was Calista Flockhart anointed the symbol of young single professional womanhood, feminism personified, by a cover story in *Time* magazine, than Ally McBeal was confronted by an obnoxious women's magazine editor, intent on putting her on the cover. Ally tells her off, naturally, reacting in a fantasy sequence by ferociously biting off her nose, then murmurs to John Cage how she dreamt she was on the cover of *Time*.

Because Peter MacNicol, who portrays Cage, plays the bagpipes, John Cage plays them as well.

And Judge Whipper Cone, the sexy older woman on the show, displays no small amount of actress Dyan Cannon's trademark independence and zest for life.

Ally McBeal Looks Like...

Audrey Hepburn, of course.

With those big eyes, the expressive lips and that occasional flicking lizard tongue...a cartoon or a puppet, too? Perhaps a big-eyed Keene waif come to life?

A long-limbed, long-necked Giacometti sculpture? An alien? Certainly, but which kind – *X-Files* or *Stargate*?

Ally McBeal does have great legs. This is an attribute she shares with Calista Flockhart, the fancifully named film and TV actress who incarnates the young Boston, Massachusetts lawyer with the vivid fantasy life and the persistent problem with self-esteem.

Of course, self-esteem is often an issue – in fact, *the* issue – for young people in the grip of anorexia nervosa or bulimia. If fictional Barrister McBeal secretly suffers from some 'eating disorder', that might explain her hallucinatory 'visions', her cute clumsiness or those abrupt, teary mood swings.

And what of the stick-thin Ms Flockhart? In the final year of the Second Millennium all the buzz in Hollywood was –

Well, at this point never mind the buzz, but the rumours did find their way into print and onto the TV chat and 'infotainment' shows that make a business of this sort of thing. Calista herself finally found it necessary to deny the rumours, both in print and on TV, that she suffered from an eating disorder. Still, the rumours persist, given additional life by the snappiness of some of her replies.

So the best one can say on the world-shaking subject of Calista Flockhart's alleged psychological problem is this: at this point, only her publicist knows for sure.

That said, there's this: *Ally McBeal* is a terrific show, with 'legs' – in the showbusiness sense – fully as long and shapely as Ms Flockhart's.

The reason for its quality does have a name: David E. Kelley, the show's protean and prolific creator, plus of course the skilled and well-meshed ensemble cast.

But like *Picket Fences* before it, *Ally McBeal* is often criticized for not having a character who acts as a moral centre. Unlike, say, *Northern Exposure*, its surrealism isn't in the service of a non-judgemental, last-frontier All-Americanism; instead, it's informed simply by a single arch stance of distanced wit and relentless sophistication.

So then, *Ally McBeal* looks like what?

The modern world?

Ally McBeal: Feminist Heroine or Pathetic Doorstop?

The real answer is neither.

Yes, she falls down a lot, taking pratfalls and having doors closed in her face on a regular basis. She's even suffered the indignity of getting stuck sitting on the toilet bowl.

But what the endless debate over What It All Means too often ignores or simply glosses over is simply this: good TV means good characters, and that means quirky, complex. Saintly, haloed role models are not necessarily the most interesting characters. Haven't we known this since Shakespeare's time at least?

Ally McBeal the show is in the tradition of magical, sometimes musical, realism. Its real antecedents are not the heroic figures of feminist history, worthy though they may be, but in the literature of the picaresque, and in such charming and quirky series as *Northern Exposure, Cop Rock, The Singing Detective* and *Pennies From Heaven,* as well as *Picket Fences,* David E. Kelley's first solo show.

The Man of Her Dreams...
Or a Dream World?

The relationship between the suggestively named Dr Greg Butters (Jesse L. Martin), a matinée-idol handsome MD, and Ally McBeal has been heating up. Whenever his back is turned, Ally's lizard tongue goes flicking out at him in one of the show's trademark surreal touches. And when she finally gets him alone, Ally, with uncharacteristic braveness, moves their relationship beyond her fervent daydreams: she confides her New Year's resolution to him ('Less fantasy, more reality!'), then gives him a passionate kiss.

That she's a white woman and he's a black man is never mentioned, just as Ling Woo (Lucy Liu) and Richard Fish (Greg Germann) never discuss their different ethnic backgrounds, or for that matter, Ally and Renee Radick never discuss theirs. Are these matter-of-fact treatments of ethnic issues a step forward or a fantastic evasion of an unpleasant truth? Could a real black man and a real white woman date and dance and kiss in public freely – and safely – in the Boston, Massachusetts of today, a cosmopolitan city to be sure, but one with a history of racial strife and intolerance as well?

Questions like these became issues for Hollywood TV-programme makers in the summer of 1999, when the NAACP (National Association for the Advancement of Colored People), a mainstream American civil-rights group, charged the TV networks with insufficient on-air diversity.

At the time, Lucy Liu, who was nominated for a Best Supporting Actress Emmy for her work on *Ally*, said (to *Daily Variety*, 27 July 1999) of the charged climate that highlighted the fact that she's one of the few Asian-Americans to appear in primetime with any regularity: 'You start putting people in categories that way. Your work should be your work...What makes the nomination so much more of an honor to me is that it's not about race, it's about what you bring to the table.'

That was a sentiment echoed (in the same article) by Jeffrey Kramer, co-executive producer on both *Ally* and *The Practice*: 'With entertainment programmes, your purpose is to entertain. When your purpose becomes other than that, you're proselytizing.'

Perhaps hard-hitting social realism is too much to expect of an avowed comedy, part satire and part fantasy, that does regularly deal with controversy, but only on its own screwball, tongue-in-cheek terms. On the other hand, even *The Cosby Show*, as mild and sweet-natured a sitcom as has ever aired, was widely credited with changing attitudes and racial stereotypes when it was broadcast in South Africa. And after all, in *ER*, to cite the most obvious example, the romance between Peter Benton (Eriq LaSalle), a black man, and Elizabeth Corday (Alex Kingston), a white British female, not only had racial overtones, but also became a public point of contention between the two actors in real life: simply put, LaSalle balked at the interracial-romance storyline, finding it unrealistic and offensive that his character's hottest on-screen moments should be with a white woman, while his relationships with black women were invariably portrayed as troubled. (As it happened, the female Afro-American character with whom Dr Benton had the most tumultuous relationship on *ER* was named Carla Reese, who was the mother of his hearing-impaired child. She was played by Lisa Nicole Carson, who also plays Renee in *Ally*.)

'We are a consciously colorblind show,' *Ally*'s protean creator told the *Los Angeles Times* in an interview (9 February 1999). 'The reason is simple. In my naive dream, I wish that the world could be like this.'

Whether or not making race a non-issue is the correct approach is debatable. But the attractiveness of the *Ally* vision is not.

Ally's Inner Life

Even without the Freudian slips and the pratfalls and the crashing into closing elevator doors, we'd still know all about exactly what it is that makes Ally so insecure.

That's because we're privy to her inner life, not only in her angst-ridden voice-over monologues and the flashbacks to her romance with Billy and to college life, but in Ally's hallucinations, her visualizing, say, the judge and jury leaping up into a gospel-tinged musical number, as well as the uncommonly rich and hip soundtrack that reflects her moods and the moods of the show. Then there are those special-effects fantasies:

When Ally feels instantly attracted to Dr Greg Butters, a handsome and debonair surgeon, we know because when she gawks open-mouthed behind his back, her lizard-like tongue snakes out at him, all the way across the room.

And when Ally feels utterly swell, ten feet tall in fact, after making out romantically with Dr Greg, we see her leaving the elevator and she is indeed so tall she's got to bend her head when she steps out. But that only lasts until the first snippy comment from Elaine, and then we see her immediately deflate. Another time, simply strolling along down a hospital corridor with Dr Greg makes her feel high, so naturally, through the magic of special effects, we see her walking nonchalantly at about his head level. But that only lasts until she unexpectedly runs into Ling, an encounter that sends her tumbling back down to earth.

When someone says something that makes her feel small, by contrast, we see her toddler-sized for a moment, in an oversized chair. And when she suspects that Georgia might be pregnant with

Billy's child, her entire face caves in. And if she knows guiltily that she back-stabbed Georgia when she kissed Billy, that, too, is illustrated by the dagger sticking out from between Georgia's shoulder blades.

And when a man she's interested in doesn't reciprocate, we know precisely how that makes Ally feel because we get a glimpse of her being thrown out of an up-ended blue dumpster bin into a garbage truck.

The Dancing Baby

Introduced in the first-season episode called 'Cro-Magnon', in which Ally also has sex with an impressively endowed male nude model, the Dancing Baby, a computer-generated special effect, quickly became the most debated media infant since Stanley Kubrick's Star Child peered down at the turning earth in the final moments of *2001*.

Critics were divided on what, exactly, it meant. Was it simply the projection of overwrought Ally's ticking biological clock or did it signal something more sinister, more anti-feminist, about her inadequacies as a modern female role model?

Whatever! There was universal agreement, though, that there was something ineffably creepy and annoying about it. With that waxy plastic doll's face, devoid of any real expression, the nappy-clad Dancing Baby looked as if at any second it might morph into Chucky and sink its fangs into Ally's leg. Let's all say it together:

Yech!

Vonda, the Music and the Dancing Twins

For a sweet little show that specializes in gentle satire, surreal fantasy and wild romanticism, *Ally McBeal* has been extraordinarily polarizing. And the most polarizing element, next to the figure of Ally herself, has been, arguably, Vonda Shepard, the singer in the bar. Is she a pallid wannabe Aretha or not?

The folky rocker with R&B soul, who plays a night-club singer named Vonda Shepard on the show, provides much of the soundtrack for Ally's inner life, performing the title tune as well as in the show's smoky night-club scenes. She once sang back-up for Jackson Browne. If that isn't a good enough musical credential, then consider this:

Her album of *Ally* music, *Songs from 'Ally McBeal', Featuring Vonda Shepard*, has sold nearly four million units world-wide, and her newest album, *By 7:30*, spins songs about unrequited love. She has released three other albums as well: *It's Good, Eve, The Radical Light* and the self-titled *Vonda Shepard*.

As for the *Ally* music itself, try a little survey. Ask the aspiring twenty-eight-year-old professional woman of your choice to hum (or nose whistle, if she's so inclined) a few bars of 'Green Onions' or sing a chorus of, say, 'The Cheater'. Odds are you'll be met with incomprehension and disbelief (if not a slap in the face). The fact is that these and the other soul- and gospel-tinged pop songs from the sixties and seventies that make up the infectious soundtrack to Ally McBeal's perplexing and problem-plagued life are, plainly, from before her time. In fact, one waits expectantly for the third, fourth or fifth season episode that will introduce the missing element in the equation: namely, the older brother (or perhaps the older never-before-mentioned lover) who first loaned young, impressionable Ally his precious record collection and thereby changed her inner life forever.

And those geeky bar habitués, the Dancing Twins? They're actually named Eric and Steve Cohen. Dressed alike, both trustworthy and dorky on the night-club dance floor, they actually started out simply enough as just two more extras on the show. But they just kept coming back and coming back, and with producers and public alike they caught on. Apparently the two brothers dress alike off stage as well.

The Mother of Invention

The ironically named Elaine Vassal is mostly comic relief, as none other than Jane Krakowski herself has attested, and yet she has had her emotional scenes too, invariably with Ally.

What's played for the biggest laughs (along with her promiscuity) is Elaine's penchant for outrageous inventions: the face bra, the automated toilet seat, the personalized condom and so on.

Mere flights of authorial whimsy? Not really. Consider:

In Japan, a 'smart' toilet is already on the market. Equipped with sensors, the toilet can monitor its user's health by analysing body waste. Would it be so much to have it equipped with a seat warmer and a remote-control seat-raising and -lowering device?

Not only that, but as a *New York Times* editorial-writer reported (28 July 1999), a company is currently advertising a new invention called a 'magnetic face mask' – which 'looks as if it had been invented by the wacky secretary Elaine on *Ally McBeal*' – and is described as increasing blood flow to tone facial muscles with 'nineteen gold-plated magnets…strategically located at your facial acupressure points'.

And yet another company which seems to have hired Elaine as a consultant is marketing a 'battery-powered suction bra [that] builds a bigger breast'. Perhaps Ling Woo will agree to produce the infomercial.

A Midsummer Night's Dream

A Midsummer Night's Dream, probably William Shakespeare's best known romantic comedy, dates from the end of the sixteenth century (it was first performed around 1595), and offers a happy and delicious blend of romance, fantasy and realism (qualities which of course could just as easily describe *Ally McBeal*) with its story of sprites and fairies and temporarily mismatched lovers. There's even a play-within-the-play that has all the low charms of vaudeville. It's a charming mix that has attracted many film-makers, including William Dieterle and Max Reinhardt, who made a delightful starry, black-and-white version in the mid thirties (the cast included James Cagney, Mickey Rooney and Olivia de Havilland), and Woody Allen, who remade it in the early eighties as *A Midsummer Night's Sex Comedy*.

In the late nineties, after the success of an adaptation of *Romeo and Juliet* that starred Leonardo DiCaprio and Claire Danes and played the Montagues and Capulets like rival gangs in a turf war, and even before the success of pictures such as the award-winning *Shakespeare In Love* and *Ten Things I Hate About You*, which set *Taming of the Shrew* in an American high school, the Bard was again all the vogue in Tinseltown.

Shakespeare even drew such thoroughly modern film stars as Alicia Silverstone, best known for her starring role in *Clueless* (which was, in fact, a clever updating of Jane Austen). She played the Princess of France in *Love's Labours Lost*, a film by Kenneth Branagh, who'd already directed and starred in *Hamlet, Henry V* and *Much Ado About Nothing*. The latter, of course, provided young actor Keanu Reaves with an excellent adventure in Shakespearian comedy.

And Jessica Lange, credible and affecting in *Rob Roy*, was taking on the role of the Queen of the Goths in *Titus*, the film adaptation of the Bard's bloodiest drama, *Titus Andronicus*.

In the summer of 1998 then, on her break from *Ally*, Calista Flockhart, who loved the stage and therefore aspired to do Shakespeare, travelled to Tuscany, in Italy, to be a part of the newest updated *Dream*. She left for the location shoot a mere two days after finishing the final episode of the TV show's second season. She recalled *(New York Times, 2 May 1999)* arriving 'jet-lagged, sort of green with exhaustion'.

Going off to work more long days on her vacation, this time clamped into period costume, was a 'no-brainer', she told the Reuters news service (12 May 1999). 'It was a lot of fun. It was like, "Go to Italy and film Shakespeare? Let me think about that."'

And, after all, it's not as if the role was that much of stretch. Helena, like Ally, is an unrequited lover, pursuing the man of her dreams, Demetrius (Christian Bale), through the enchanted wood, and doing pratfalls (albeit from a bicycle).

This *Dream*, like Woody Allen's delightful romp, was set around the turn of the nineteenth century, and its characters wore straw boaters and dresses with bustles and sped around the magical wood on bikes. The $13.5 million production, directed by Michael Hoffman, probably best known for the period drama *Restoration*, had a dream of a cast too, that included Kevin Kline (as braying Bottom), Rupert Everett (Oberon, the Fairy King), David Strathairn (Duke Theseus) and Stanley Tucci, who as Puck gets to oversee the merriment and deliver that famous 'Lord, what fools these mortals be!' speech.

Calista played Helena and Mrs David E. Kelley, better known to film audiences as Michelle Pfeiffer, played Titania, the Queen of the Fairies.

That Calista Flockhart and Michelle Pfeiffer – probably the movie's two most 'bankable' stars – had no scenes together, and in fact weren't even on location at the same time, was little remarked upon. Or if it was, it was dismissed with a shrug – after all, any big film production, with forty days on location, might have more than one such scheduling quirk.

Was it true or not? (Unfortunately, Gentle Reader, one raises the question not to provide edification, but out of a sense of what the marketplace wants.)

In the hot-house atmosphere of a hit TV series, shooting on a closed sound stage – with highly strung, creative people thrown together fourteen hours a day, five or six days a week, week in and week out – such things have been known to happen. But beyond the gossip itself, there is absolutely no evidence for it.

The movie itself opened almost a year later to less than overwhelmed reviews. Typical was the reaction of the influential *New York Times* (14 May 1999), which called the production 'fussy' and a 'hodgepodge', and said of the performances that they ranged from the 'sublime to the you-know-what'.

Playing the Fairy Queen, Michelle Pfeiffer was commanding and lovely, wrote Janet Maslin, the *Times* reviewer, while Calista played the distraught Helena as a 'hand-waving, eye-rolling ditz'. Another writer called her portrayal of the 'masochistic Helena as Ally McBeal less law degree: not just a flake but a year's supply of Ivory Snow'.

To what extent she'd been commanded to play the part that way, and to what extent The Actress had been infected by The Character she played on television is, of course, impossible to sort out.

The Danger of the TV Actor's Life

'I think they've actually done studies on the psychological effects on actors playing the same part for a long time. I don't know what the conclusion was. It probably said that they go insane and have identity crises.' – Calista Flockhart, *Los Angeles* magazine, June 1999.

How She Finds the Character

Some actors swear by the Method, perhaps imagining a detailed back story to explain the character's actions and motivations. Others may resort to more private methods.

For actresses particularly, one of the most sensible-sounding ploys is to draw the portrayal from the way the character dresses, from the costume and its peculiarities. And the most sensible-sounding method of all is to begin with the shoes, which is exactly how she learns about more than just a character's gait.

'I'm a big believer in shoes,' Calista said (*New York Times*, 2 May 1999). 'They can, like, tell you who exactly your character is.'

A Risky Move

It was the cruellest month, April, and the New York theatre world was 'ablaze' with a rumour, according to *Variety* (16 April 1999): Calista Flockhart, who was at the time subject to public and press speculation on a grand scale, was 'hungry' to return to her roots in theatre, perhaps as soon as her summer production break from *Ally*. She'd been offered a starring role in a revival of John van Druten's *I Am a Camera*, according to the rumour. The play was based on Christopher Isherwood's *The Berlin Stories*: 'The Last of Mr Norris' and 'Goodbye to Berlin', which in turn was the basis of the musical *Cabaret*. Would it then be Calista as Sally Bowles?

She would rehearse for three weeks, then appear on stage for five, but – according to another version of the rumour – the play would not be *I Am a Camera*; it would be William Mastrosimone's *The Woolgatherer* instead.

A little more than a month later, *Variety*, which is always hungry for a scoop, had got the real inside information: a deal was 'imminent' for Calista to appear off-Broadway, in the relatively tiny, 199-seat Douglas Fairbanks Theater, in a triptych of one-act plays written by Neil LaBute.

LaBute was best known as the writer–director of two bleak and controversial films, *In the Company of Men* and *Your Friends and Neighbors*, which offered up harsh and closely observed views of the modern relationships between men and women. The men in LaBute's movies were generally misogynistic and predatory, or they were dupes, and more often than not the women were unhappy and alone, or they were prey. Perceptive essayist and critic John Lahr called LaBute the 'best new playwright to emerge in the past decade'.

The three one-act monologues went by the overall title of *A Gaggle of Saints*, said the trade paper, and Calista would appear in two.

The first would be 'Bash', about gay-bashing, while 'Medea Redux' and 'Iphegenia in Orem' were modern variations of the well-known tales from Greek mythology – about a princess wise in the ways of sorcery, and the daughter of King Agamemnon, respectively.

The one-act plays would be performed by just three actors – Calista, Ron Eldard and Paul Rudd – and were to be directed by Joe Mantello.

By the time the curtain actually went up, in late June, there was a new title, *Bash, Latterday Plays*, and Calista was now firmly established as the most prominent example of a new trend: the TV actor as a theatrical drawing card.

On the New York stage that summer were also Tony Danza, best known for his role as one of the colourful cabbies in *Taxi* (in *The Iceman Cometh*); Bill Brochtrup, who played the homosexual station-house aide in *NYPD Blue* (in *Snakebit*, off-Broadway); Polly Draper, best known for her role as Ellen in *Thirtysomething* (in *Closer*); George Segal, who played the self-centred magazine publisher in *Just Shoot Me*, a half-hour situation comedy set in a *Cosmo*-like magazine (in *Art*, a three-man play on Broadway); and Wayne Knight, who played the postman in *Seinfeld* and then switched to a police uniform for a supporting role in *Third Rock from the Sun* (also in *Art*).

There was even another actress from a David E. Kelley series treading the boards off-Broadway: Lisa Gay Hamilton, who played Rebecca Washington in *The Practice*, had taken the lead role in *Angelique*, a period drama about a slave, and she was drawing rave reviews.

But clearly the most closely watched, and the biggest draw of them all, would be the other actress from the other David E. Kelley series, The Actress at the Centre of All the Controversy.

The theatrical evening began with the spotlight fixed both metaphorically and actually on Flockhart, who played a jilted lover in 'Medea Redux', the opening one-acter, seated alone at a plain table. Like the second playlet, 'Iphegenia in Orem', in which Ron Eldard took the stage, 'Medea' turned on the revelation of a horrific crime, the murder of a child by a parent.

In the third one-acter, now entitled 'A Gaggle of Saints', Flockhart returned as one of two Mormon college students (Paul Rudd played the other) in New York for a weekend, who become involved in a horrific gay-bashing.

In the circumstances the stage, which she so loved, had become a precipice, and for the notoriously tough-minded New York critics nothing could have been easier than knocking her off.

The jokes were ready to hand. In the words of one wag, 'bash' was just what the critics would do to the nervy young actress; in the words of another, the critics were lying in wait to eat her alive.

Vindication

It was a gamble and it paid off. On a late June morning, Calista Flockhart, mauled and much maligned in the press for months, awoke to rave reviews. *Variety*'s review (24 June 1999) is worth quoting at length:

> [Calista Flockhart] reveals talents little used in her role as the fey attorney on the Fox TV show: a quietly seething intensity, a captivating and, yes, delicate physical presence, a natural command of the stage that seduces the audience's sympathy...
>
> Flockhart's tremulous air, her fluttering hands and gauntly lit features (accentuated in James Vermeulen's stylish, harshly dramatic lighting) lend an air of disturbing authenticity...
>
> Flockhart's performance is so fine she ultimately transcends the patly horrific ending...letting out a howl of despair and rage that is so pure and profoundly felt it lends its own, harrowing truth to the play – a volley of anguish untethered to the narrative that reveals an actress who can communicate wells of pain that reach deeper than the text does.

Some critics liked all of *Bash*, others liked one or another of the playlets, but not all three; but the praise for Calista's performance, both by critics who knew of her past as a stage actress and those who did not, was universal. From other important critics, both from New York and the national press, who joined the extravagant chorus, were these words of unqualified praise:

'Ms Flockhart, by the magnitude of her stardom, had more to lose than most television stars in hazarding a return to the stage. She had a potent weapon, though; she can act...[Her portrayal in 'Medea Redux'] is so alive that you imagine her in motion constantly, when in fact she is glued to the interview table.' (*New York Times*, 2 July 1999)

She 'slums credibly', said the drama critic for the Associated Press, 'projecting a realistic low-class demeanor. She is not afraid to put herself out on a limb, even to the point of transforming herself physically into one scary-looking woman.'

And from *USA Today*, the newspaper known for its short news features and 'freeze-dried TV' style, came this about Calista Flockhart's performance in 'Medea': 'Spellbinding.'

Back in the broader world of TV Land, the final episode of the show's second season had stirred up all the criticism about lovelorn Ally as an unsuitable role model. But by the end of the last summer of the century, the criticism had abated somewhat. In any case, it seemed that Calista herself had moved on, taking a role in *Things You Can Tell Just by Looking at Her*, a small-budget, big-screen romantic comedy that, according to a Reuters report, interwove several stories of 'love and loss', and also starred Cameron Diaz, Glenn Close, Holly Hunter, Kathy Baker and Gregory Hines. And at the 1999 Emmys, the premier American TV excellence awards, given out by the Academy of Television Arts & Sciences, *Ally McBeal* received the most nominations of any comedy series, including a nomination for Calista Flockhart as Outstanding Actress in a Comedy.

And in an *Ally*-worthy irony, the series tied with *The Practice* for most nominations of any non-cable series. (Also honoured with a lucky thirteen nominations was a miniseries – *Joan of Arc* – which recounted the adventures of another dreamy young woman who saw visions and suffered.)

The New, Thinner Ally

David E. Kelley had a stunningly unconventional response to an unpleasant fact of life in the television business, and Fox, the avowedly unconventional network that aired his *Ally McBeal*, was just the place to try it out.

The unpleasant fact of life was this: one-hour dramas earn significantly less money in domestic syndication in the United States than do half-hour situation comedies. Hour dramas earn less for a number of reasons – some cyclical, others endemic to the business. The stations that buy syndicated programming often have mostly half-hour slots to fill; the fewer one-hour slots available mean that relatively few one-hour dramas on the market constitute a glut; a half-hour comedy, which often depends more on jokes than a story, tends to repeat better in the ratings and to travel well; an hour drama, on the other hand, which often involves plot twists and a fourth-act revelation, tends to wear out its welcome once the viewer knows what the individual episode ahead holds.

What makes this so unspeakably important to the creators and owners of television programmes is something called 'deficit financing', which is the widespread practice of spending more to produce a programme than the US network originally pays to air it. The need to absorb the deficit is the bitterest complaint of any Hollywood TV producer. What makes deficit financing acceptable at all is that after its original network run a show will go into domestic (and international) syndication.

And that's when the money – usually pure profit after the deficit is covered – pours in. So lower fees for one-hour dramas meant, quite simply, money out of Mr Kelley's pocket.

That's when he came up with his unconventional idea: take those already aired *Ally McBeal* episodes, remix and recut them with never-aired footage and – voila! – half-hour episodes of a new, 'thinner' version of the same show, to be called simply *Ally*, which would have a new musical theme and would air weekly one day after the original one-hour version of the show. The half-hour *Ally* would concentrate on the personal relationships and the firm, and would de-emphasize the courtroom aspects of the one-hour show. And as a bonus for the network the new version would be cheaper to air than a new series.

It was breathtakingly simple, and yet no one could remember it ever having been done before. And of course it would be the new half-hour version that would go out to syndication, where it would presumably command those higher half-hour-sitcom rates.

Of all the broadcast television networks that Kelley could have approached to try his experiment, it was probably Fox that was the most natural and receptive place. And that was partly because Fox, the so-called Fourth Network in the United States, aired *Ally McBeal*, while Fox, the studio, produced it. And both Foxes were divisions of the News Corporation, a most singular international conglomerate. Its newspapers – in particular, the *National Star*, the *New York Post* and the *Sun* in London – were best known for a brazen tabloid style that included cheesecake photos of pretty, sometimes bare-breasted, girls. News Corp. also delivered satellite programming to Britain, across Asia and elsewhere.

In the United States, in addition to the Fox broadcast network, the one that aired *Ally McBeal*, it owned several other cable networks, including a number of regional all-sports networks, a Spanish-language sports network, an all-news channel, the Fox Family Channel and FX, a cable channel aimed at young male viewers. Nightly, FX offered such shows as *NYPD Blue*, *The X-Files*, *MASH* and *Millennium*.

Around the same time that Kelley was offering the Fox broadcast network his vision of a half-hour *Ally*, showing them five sample half-hour shows that he'd put together on his own, FX shocked the rest of the cable industry by suddenly buying the syndication rights to the one-hour *Ally McBeal*, as well as to *The Practice*, Kelley's other Boston lawyer show.

According to one trade-paper report (*Variety*, 9 June 1999) by uncommonly knowledgeable writers, FX was paying about $650,000 an hour for *The Practice* over the life of the contract, and about $750,000 an episode for *Ally McBeal*. Although it was a deal between two divisions of the same company, one paying into the coffers of the other, it was worth overall an estimated $370 million, according to the report.

What left cable operators and others 'dazed and confused', as the report put it, was the widespread perception that *Ally McBeal* was a show that appealed primarily to young women, while FX was a network that had consciously declared that its strategy was to appeal to men aged eighteen to thirty-four.

The response of the network was that *Ally McBeal* attracted 'hip, savvy, cynical' viewers of both sexes, and that was just fine with FX.

In the United States a full television year runs from September to May, with the summer traditionally given over to repeats. In the 1997–8 season, when *Ally McBeal* debuted, it was an immediate success with the critics and a 'water-cooler', or word-of-mouth, hit with the public, building up that coveted hip, young audience.

In the 1998–9 season, its popularity grew further, even as the good qualities of the show itself threatened to be overshadowed by the Is She or Isn't She (Anorexic, a Fit Feminist Role Model) controversies.

And then, on the very verge of the United States' 1999–2000 TV season, arguably the hottest and most eagerly anticipated new show on television was an improbable little sitcom named…

Ally.

The Guide
to the Show

The Cast and the Characters

*Calista Flockhart plays Ally McBeal, the young,
Harvard-trained Boston attorney whose firm employs
not only her ex-college boyfriend, the love of her life,
but his beautiful wife as well.*

You might think Ally's life centres around her busy calendar of court cases, but it's really her social life and her own hyperactive imaginings with which she's obsessed.

Calista Flockhart, a stage actress, makes her primetime-series debut in this series. Immediately prior to *Ally*, she was on Broadway as Natasha in Scott Elliot's acclaimed production of *The Three Sisters*.

She made her Broadway debut opposite Julie Harris in *The Glass Menagerie*, for which she won the Theater World Award and the Clarence Derwent Best New Talent Award. Additional New York theatre credits include *The Loop*, which landed her the role of Barbara in *The Birdcage*; *Sophistry and Sons* and *Fathers*, both opposite Ethan Hawke; Garry Marshall's *Wrong Turn at Lungfish*; *All For One* with Liev Schrieber; and Caryl Churchill's *Mad Forest*.

Regional theatre includes Juliet in *Romeo and Juliet*, Cordelia in *King Lear*, Irina in *The Three Sisters* and Emily in *Our Town*, which was directed by the legendary Jose Quintero. Summers at the Williamstown Theater Festival and the Berkshire Theater Festival include roles in *Death Takes a Holiday* opposite Christopher Reeve, and *Jittas Atonement* opposite Dianne Wiest.

Her feature film credits include *Drunks*, *Telling Lies in America* and *The Birdcage*, which received the Screen Actors Guild Award for Best Ensemble.

Flockhart was born in Illinois.

Gil Bellows plays Billy Alan Thomas, quizzical and earnest, Ally's former boyfriend and current colleague.

Billy loves his wife, the beautiful Georgia, without one single doubt. They've even been caught doing 'it' in the firm's unisex loo. But there's Ally, always mooning about, doing ever-so-cute pratfalls and double takes, so sincerely searching, yearning – is it any wonder that a certain look of, well, possibility cross his Baldwin-handsome face from time to time.

'Billy' may be the most thankless male role on series TV. Sometimes Bellows looks trapped in a mostly decorative part that only calls for him to look good and display an emotional range that runs all the way from earnest adoration to earnest confusion.

Gil Bellows's television credits include co-starring with Kirstie Alley in the Hallmark Hall of Fame movie *Radiant City*, and the series *Law & Order* and *Going to Extremes*.

He has appeared in the feature films *Miami Rhapsody*, *Love and a .45*, *The Shawshank Redemption*, *White Lies* and *Richard III*, which was directed by Al Pacino. His theatre credits include *A Snake in the Vein*, *Best of Schools*, *King Lear* and *Diary of Anne Frank*.

Bellows was born and raised in Vancouver. He graduated from the American Academy of Dramatic Arts in Los Angeles. He is married and lives in Los Angeles.

Courtney Thorne-Smith plays Georgia Thomas, Billy's wife. You would expect mad jealousy and operatic hate, but as much as Ally and Georgia want to dislike each other, they simply can't. Georgia is intelligent, beautiful, virtuous, and Ally can't help seeing that.

They feel sisterly affection, as if they shared the 'same DNA, but it's Billy's'.

Courtney Thorne-Smith starred as Alison Parker in *Melrose Place* for five years. Her other television series regular credits include *Day By Day* and *Fast Times at Ridgemont High*, as well as a recurring role on *LA Law* and a guest star appearance in *Anything But Love*. Thorne-Smith also starred in the telefilms *Beauty's Revenge* and *Tour of Duty*.

Her feature film credits include *Lucas, Summer School, Revenge of the Nerds II* and the upcoming *Chairman of the Board*, which opens in autumn 1999.

She began her career during her senior year in high school with The Ensemble Theatre Company in Mill Valley, California.

Born in San Francisco, Thorne-Smith is single and resides in Los Angeles.

Greg Germann plays Richard Fish, Ally's former law-school mate and now one of the two principals of her firm, Cage/Fish & Associates.

Richard has contrarian opinions, a way with words and a matter-of-fact disdain for the proprieties that keep most people from speaking their minds. But for self-aware and purposefully insensitive guy Richard Fish, it's all just a professional strategy – he plays God after all – and it all just amounts to, well . . . bygones.

Greg Germann most recently co-starred for two seasons in *Ned and Stacey* as Eric, Ned's best friend. He was born in Houston and raised in Colorado, later attending the University of Northern Colorado, where he majored in theatre.

Upon graduating, he moved to New York, where he became a member of the Circle Rep and Ensemble Studio Theatre.

Germann's New York theatre credits include such off-Broadway and Broadway plays as *New York Actor* and the Stephen Sondheim musical *Assassins*.

His television credits include such series such as *Sweet Justice*, *These Friends of Mine*, *Tour of Duty* and *Against the Law*. He has also appeared as a guest star on *LA Law*, *Bakersfield PD* and the movie *Conduct Unbecoming*.

In feature films, his credits include *IQ*, *Clear and Present Danger*, *So I Married an Axe Murderer*, *Once Around* and *Miss Firecracker*. He has also recently completed the short film *Pete's Garden*, which he wrote, directed and starred in.

Germann, who is married to actress Christine Mourad, splits his time between New York and Los Angeles.

Peter MacNicol plays John Cage, the shy boy-man with the manner of a Zen adept – a Zen adept, that is, who is a herpetologist and gymnast as well.

MacNicol's career has ranged from the drama of television series *Chicago Hope* to the comedy of *Ghostbusters 2* and *Bean*.

He made his film debut as the young Southern writer in love with Meryl Streep in *Sophie's Choice*. His other credits include *Adams Family Values*, *Dracula: Dead and Loving It*, *Housesitter*, *Hard Promises* and *Heat*.

For television, MacNicol has also starred in the series *The Powers That Be*, as well as the telefilms *Abducted: A Father's Love* and *By the Dawn's Early Light*. On stage, he starred on Broadway in *Crimes of the Heart*, *Black Comedy/White Liars* and *The Nerd*. He has also starred in New York Shakespeare Festival productions of *Romeo and Juliet*, *Richard II* and *Twelfth Night*, as well as *Found a Peanut* and *Rum and Coke*.

He was born in Texas. He resides in Los Angeles with his wife Marsue.

Lisa Nicole Carson plays Renee Radick, Ally's room-mate with the infectious smile. She is also a prosecutor who may oppose Ally in court but always supports her in dealing with the chaos and angst of her private live.

Lisa Nicole Carson's television credits include the series *ER* (on which she has the recurring role of Carla, the mother of Dr Peter Benton's child), *Divas, Girlfriend* and *The Apollo Comedy Hour*.

She has appeared in the feature films *Love Jones, Devil In A Blue Dress, Jason's Lyric*, and *Eve's Bayou*. Her theatre credits include *Club 12, Hey Little Walter, Little Shop of Horrors, Tar Beach Incidentals* and *Work It!*

Born in Brooklyn, New York, she now resides Los Angeles and New York.

Jane Krakowski plays Elaine Vassal, Ally's personal assistant, an unabashed busybody and truth-teller. She's an inveterate schemer too, apt to come up with some unlikely contraption such as the face bra, the personalized condom or the remote-controlled toilet seat, when she's not enthusiastically throwing herself at men.

Her television work includes *Early Edition, Due South, The High Life, Great Performances 20th Anniversary Special, Young Indiana Jones, Queen, Return to Kansas City, Against the Law, When We Were Young* and *Search for Tomorrow*, for which she was nominated for two Emmy Awards.

Her film credits include *Shut Up and Dance, Hudson River Blues, Mrs Winterbourne, Stepping Out, Fatal Attraction* and *National Lampoon's Vacation*.

She has appeared in several Broadway productions, including *Once Upon a Mattress, Tartuffe, Company, Face Value, Starlight Express* and *Grand Hotel*, for which she was nominated for a Tony Award and a Drama Desk Award. Krakowski's other theatre work includes *Encores! One Touch of Venus* and *Henceforward,* for which she received an LA Drama Critic Award as Best Actress.

She can also be heard on Verese Saraband's latest recordings *Lost in Boston IV* and *Sondheim at the Movies,* the soundtrack for the independent film *Hudson River Blues* and many other Broadway original cast recordings of the shows in which she has appeared.

Born in New Jersey, she now resides in New York and Los Angeles.

Portia de Rossi plays 'Sub-Zero' Nelle Porter, the stunning, white-blonde-maned attorney with the cool demeanour, the tough reputation and the warm heart who – improbably but winningly – is attracted to meek John Cage.

Her film credits include *Stigmata, American Intellectuals, Girl, Scream 2* and *Sirens.* Her television work includes *Nick Freno: Licensed Teacher* and *Too Something.*

Lucy Liu plays Ling Woo, simultaneously Cage/Fish's most intriguing and annoying client, as well as more recently one of its 'of counsel' associates. Ling, a woman of many talents and enterprises, is also carrying on an oh-so-cool, two-scorpions-in-the-bottle affair with Richard Fish.

So incredible are Ling's love-making techniques that she makes Richard sign a non-disclosure agreement before they go to bed, and her finger-licking and hair-flicking foreplay demonstrates convincingly that men have more than just the one 'dumb stick'.

Liu's credits include *Shanghai Noon, True Crime, Payback, Molly, City of Industry, Gridlock'd* and *Jerry Maguire.* Her TV work includes *Riot* and *Pearl.*

Dyan Cannon plays Jennifer 'Whipper' Cone,
a judge who's cool and self-possessed on the bench, but
as neurotic and conflicted as anyone else in her private life. It's a
condition that was no doubt exacerbated by the brief affair she
once had with Richard Fish.

Cannon's many film and TV credits include *Kiss of a Stranger, Out to Sea, Eight Heads in a Duffel Bag, That Darn Cat, The Pickle, The End of Innocence, Deathtrap, Honeysuckle Rose, Revenge of the Pink Panther, Heaven Can Wait, The Virginia Hill Story, The Last of Sheila, The Anderson Tapes, Bob & Carol & Ted & Alice* and *The Rise and Fall of Legs Diamond.*

Fishisms and Other Allyisms

He's not just a callous and shallow yuppie lawyer whose avowed aspiration is to make 'piles and piles of money'. Richard Fish is a philosopher too. These are a few of his thoughts:

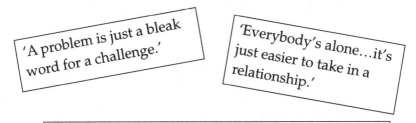

'A problem is just a bleak word for a challenge.'

'Everybody's alone…it's just easier to take in a relationship.'

'Bygones' – by which he pithily sums up and characteristically dismisses all no-longer-profitable emotions and conversations.

Richard Fish Esquire is hardly the only member of the firm with a flair for words – thanks, of course, to the writing of David E. Kelley. Even Ally herself, so tongue-tied at all the most crucial moments in her personal life ('Eat me,' she blithers Freudian-like, upon meeting one handsome young man), will deliver the occasional memorable *bon mot*. More examples from the files of Cage/Fish & Associates follow:

'So here I am the victim of my own choices, and I'm just starting.' (Ally)

'Love and law are the same, romantic in concept, but the actual practice can get you a yeast infection.' (Ally)

'Seriously, is working with Billy going to be a problem? Because if it is, well then I can't do anything about it, but you know I'd be happy to sympathize.' (Richard to Ally)

'Let me tell you something, I didn't become a lawyer because I like the law, the law sucks. It's boring, but it can also be used as a weapon. You want to bankrupt somebody? Cost him everything he's worked for? Make his wife leave him, even make his kids cry? Yeah, we can do that.' (Richard, of course)

'Love, you can't bank on it...The only thing you can bring to the bank [is] money.' (Richard)

'Today is going be an, uh, a less bad day. I can feel it. Sometimes I wake up and I just know that everything is going to be...less bad.' (Ally)

'It doesn't matter that I'm not in a relationship with anybody. Sometimes I feel like I'm being unfaithful to love itself.' (Ally)

'Where does it say that women can't act like men sometimes? I saw a piece of cute meat, and I said to myself, "You only live once: be a man."' (Ally)

'It's not easy to meet women. Sure I can walk into a bar and buy a lady a drink and under the pretext of a perhaps budding relationship seduce her into satisfying my sexual needs. But that goes against my grain, to deceive another person no matter what the physical gratification. So I thought it more honest to solicit a prostitute.' (John)

'John, a second of your time. We started this firm with the same dream, did we not?'

'Money.'

'In pursuit of that dream we agreed that I would be the shark, the hammer, the ass, and you would be the pillar of dignity. This was the deal. Have I not been every bit the ass you envisioned?'

'And more.'

'It escapes me as to how soliciting hookers fits into your scheme, but instead of belabouring it, I'd like to focus on the positive. The fact is that when a person reveals a flaw, he often does so by digging deeper into himself. What happened to you can only build character. John, you are a stronger man today than you were yesterday. I can even feel it just standing next to you. Just feel it. The strength! Well done!'

(Richard and John)

'Whoever said that plenty-of-fish-in-the-sea thing was lying. Sometimes there's only one fish. Trust me.' (Ally)

'I think I need to believe that it works – love, couplehood, partnerships. The idea that when people come together, they stay together. I have to take that with me to bed, even if I have to go to bed alone.' (Ally)

'Maybe it's because they say love is about learning to compromise, that's why they get themselves into compromising positions. They can call it research.' (Ally)

'The first dance is critical. I never start off close. It gives me no place to go. A dance is basically foreplay. First there is the smile, then the laugh. The right kind of laugh can make a man feel interesting and funny. And that's what guys love most in women. Somebody who makes them feel engaging. I'm not listening to a word he says. And he's not hearing anything I say. He's got two questions: Does she like me and will my mother like her? This is the part where you just hold his eyes, look right at him, give him a sense of progress, I think I'll get closer now. Let him smell me. Little smile, little sniff – it's so easy.' (Ally)

'What, he can't be a man and just palm me a little? I'm a sexual object, for god's sake! What, he can't give me a little grope?' (Ally)

'It's not my style to care about others, but, what's going on?' (Richard)

'A face bra. Next to ageing and sun exposure, jogging is one of the leading causes of wrinkles. The up and down motion breaks down the skin's elasticity. This holds the face in place.' (Elaine)

'This [funeral] will be like a class reunion. Instead of a punch bowl, there's a coffin. But remember, reunions are meant to allow the more successful graduates to inform the less successful that that's what they are: less than. You and I, we're more than. Especially me. Me, I have my own firm. I could possibly be the most. My point is, life is about attitude. And tonight is a night for you to feel good about yourself.' (Richard)

'One of the keys to life: the fast forward. Every movie has its lousy parts. The trick is to fast forward through them. As time passes, you look back and say, "Oh that little adultery thing, oh that." You fast-forward to right now, and you're over it.' (Richard)

'You pissy little thing, pushing your little cart in your Calvin Klein outfit! You probably only choose those chips because I left them on the edge, and you won't have to pop a pore to reach them.' (a female customer in a grocery store, arguing with Ally over potato crisps)

'Just remember, when I'm here you're not the strangest person in the room. Go ahead, get weird on me.' (Ally to John)

'Hi, I'm Ally McBeat, Meat, Meal, Beal! Ally McBeal. It takes a while, but I usually get it right.' (Ally introducing herself to a man)

'Don't ask questions, don't pass judgement, don't even pass go, just listen and accept the fact that I need help and give it to me.' (Ally)

'I am nothing if not surrounded.' (Richard)

'Of course I talk about [Ally], I talk about her all the time. I also have allergies, but I would be at a loss to recall a specific sneeze.' (Elaine)

'I'm sure she is quite stupid and in time gravity will get her.' (Elaine)

'I'll go gather myself.' (John)

'Comfort is good.' (Ally)

'The sad thing is, in a movie we'd both be rooting for the gal to date the guy.' (Renee)

'The world is no longer a romantic place, some of its people still are, however, and therein lies the promise. Don't let the world win, Ally McBeal.' (John)

'Just pop it.'

'I don't want to pop it, it could swell. You don't want enlarged pores on the first date. There. I diminished it.'

'What do you mean, diminished it?'

'I've diminished the pimple.'

'What are you doing?'

'Ally has a date tonight and I'm minimizing her facial flaws.'

'What? Are you always such a bitchy little thing? Coming in here insulting the Torah, insulting me.' (a rabbi to Ally)

'God has no love for the bitchy?' (Ally to the rabbi)

'That's the thing about me. I make all my clients forget about all their troubles by giving them bigger ones.' (Ally)

'I have a thing about first impressions. I will forever see him as salad-dressing face.' (Ally)

'Like it or not, you would be unhireable. That's not a real word, I use it anyway, which should give you an idea of how severely it applies.' (John)

'I demand to know what part of me you are laughing at.' (Ally)

'I hate it when I don't know what I've done, especially if it's something good. I demand to know why you are pleased with me!' (Ally)

'Helping people is never more rewarding, especially if it's in your own self-interest.' (Richard)

'Miss you at every opportunity, Elaine. Kidding. Bygones. Go away.' (Richard)

'With all due respect, you sort of walk around with uppity breasts, and the hair flips aren't the most subtle. Your perfume, you could be flammable. Now what if somebody shut you down as a safety hazard, how would you feel then?' (Ally)

'Would you mind turning on the faucet? I have a bashful bladder.' (Ally)

'It's not a good feeling to be married to a person who I am in love with and still not be over another.' (Billy)

'Emotionally, you're an idiot.' (Renee to Ally)

'When you make love to a guy do you look him in the eyes?'

'If our heads are on the same side of the bed, I most certainly do.'

'As long as we are drawing lines, do you think it would be possible for you to, you know, not feign orgasms in the office?' (Billy to Ally)

'I plan to have character one day, great character, but if you want to be rich, you better get the money before the scruples set in, that's a, you know...'

'Fishism.'

'I am an enigma.' (John)

'You're a cute little enigma.' (Renee)

'Freefall with the truth, hope we both survive, deal?' (Ally to Billy)

'Cruelty is funny to you? Pain?'

'When it's someone else's.'

'You know what, Renee? Bite me.'

'You know, I had a great aunt who once said, "If you stare at a beautiful woman too long, you turn to stone." She was partially right.' (Richard)

'New firm policy, listen up. Anybody who sues this firm, or me personally, we all drop whatever cases we are working on and devote all our intellectual and creative efforts to ruining that person's life. Are we clear? I do not want to stop short with getting even. Retribution? Not strong enough. Ruin! That's the goal. Irreversible, irreparable, irrational ruin. New firm policy.' (Richard)

'But in your lawsuit you demanded that she be terminated.'

'That was an alternative demand. The first demand was that she would stop walking around in her slutty little way.'

'Do you make room for the slightest possibility that she might feel the least bit oppressed?'

'Well, if she felt that way, she shouldn't dress how she dresses, flaunting her big alabaster boobies in everybody's faces.'

'Selfishism.' (Richard, describing the firm's philosophy)

Ally on the Web

Great sites on the Web can go missing and founts of timely information can, with no notice, crash or simply fizzle to a dead stop. Such are the risks of cyberspace, where everything is in flux. But fortunately, everything in cyberspace is connected, too. For those of you who might not know, the trick of finding information on the Internet, without spending what will soon seem like an endless summer surfing the Web, is to find a convenient and efficient jumping-off point.

Among the jewels of the Web, an excellent general first stop whenever you want any entertainment-related information, whether about a person, a movie or a show, is the Internet Movie Database, which you will find at **http://uk.imdb.com**.

At last count, there were no fewer than 16,813 Web pages for 'Ally McBeal'. Enter 'Calista Flockhart' at your favourite search engine and something like 5,777 pages or so will come up. (By comparison, for 'David E. Kelley' there are 1,552 pages on the World Wide Web.) If your interest is in information about *Ally McBeal*, you just might want to start at the official site, Foxworld, which you'll find at **http://www.foxworld.com**.

Among the many unofficial sites, one of the best at the time of writing is **http://wonko.inow.com/wilco/entertainment/allymcbeal/links.html**, where you will find links to many of the most comprehensive and dedicated fan sites.

The First Season

The Pilot

There is a reason that *Ally McBeal*, the one-hour comedy-drama show, was drafted originally by Fox TV executives to fill the timeslot immediately after *Melrose Place*. And that reason is on display right from the very first episode, in which Ally, a twenty-seven-year-old Harvard-trained lawyer is sexually harassed at her old firm and then signs on with Cage/Fish & Associates.

From the absolute get-go it was clear that the show was most definitely a glossy, upscale, hip, young…soap opera, albeit written and acted at an uncommonly high level of quality.

Someone just tuning in to the pilot episode could be forgiven for thinking Aaron Spelling, the producer of *Melrose*, had simply traded trendy LA for trendy Boston. After all, there were still beauties in miniskirts, model-handsome young guys, glamorous doings and digs, passionate trysts, and plenty of good old-fashioned S–E–X. There was even Courtney Thorne-Smith.

But this was much more than the standard *Melrose* melodramatics or the usual heavy-breathing fluff of a typical Aaron Spelling series.

For one thing, there is Ally's rich fantasy life and her novelistic interior monologues. These are on abundant display in the very first episode. David E. Kelley's quirky visual sensibility and evident fondness for what in literature is called 'magical realism', as well as for visual and auditory puns, made it evident from the start that this soap was on different plane (if not a different planet) to *Melrose Place*.

From the first episode on, then, when young lawyer Ally McBeal experiences emotional turmoil – which is guaranteed when she takes that job at Cage/Fish & Associates, the very firm where her childhood sweetheart and first love also works – we, the viewers, see and hear it all.

The fantasy special effects that do so much to set this show apart, and are the external manifestations of Ally's inner life, are generally charming...but they can grate and be cloying. After all, how many times do you want to see that flicking lizard tongue, the garbage truck that symbolizes rejection or the creepy Dancing Baby? But that's later.

The first episode alone has Ally and Billy having sex in a giant cup of latte, Elaine's head swelling up, Ally's breasts ballooning alarmingly and so many arrows piercing Ally's heart that she looks like Toshiro Mifune at the end of Akira Kurosawa's aptly-named *Throne of Blood*.

For more ambience there are the songs of Vonda Shepard, who looks remarkably like Carly Simon and sounds like a cross between her and Dionne Warwick, and who mixes an 'Anticipation'-like, lovelorn and angst-ridden middle-of-the-road pop (the kind of songs Ol' Blue Eyes might have sung) with sixties rhythm-and-blues, those great Motown songs, like 'Tell Him'.

In the pilot, in voice-over and flashback, young lawyer Ally McBeal recalls how she initially went to law school to follow her childhood sweetheart, Billy Alan Thomas, to Harvard. Through Ally's recollection we see her and Billy as seven-year-olds and as teens. We learn that from early childhood Ally connected with Billy on the pheromone level: she liked how he smelled.

In school they broke up and Billy transferred to Michigan (he had already met Georgia, who went there, but in the pilot episode Ally doesn't know that), but Ally carried on in Boston to become a lawyer with a prominent firm there, finally leaving because a partner was harassing her.

Then Ally gets the new job that sets the show into forward motion: joining the firm headed by an old classmate: money-loving, politically incorrect Richard Fish, who gives Ally her first case, defending a magazine in a censorship case. It's the first of many cases touching on matters sexual and romantic that come to Ally at Cage/Fish & Associates.

She also meets her new secretary, Elaine Vassal, whose efficiency is matched only by her gleeful inquisitiveness about Ally's (and everyone else's) personal life.

And Ally meets another of the firm's young associates, who just happens to turn out to be…her One True Love, Billy Alan Thomas, and he just happens to be… well, the next morning Ally finally learns that Billy is married.

In the meantime, Fish recommends that Billy handle Ally's sexual-harassment case.

Ally tries to act as if nothing has changed, but Renee, her roommate, knows better – that working with Billy will be trying in the extreme. It's not the last time that Renee Radick will offer Ally such sage advice.

At the office the next morning, Fish tells Ally about an upcoming meeting with a prospective client, Air National. Billy reveals to Ally that he is now married.

Ally tries to hide her disappointment, but is soon making an angry, and inappropriate, remark to a stranger on the street. To Ally's amazement, at trial the judge rules against her client, although he does invite her to appeal.

When Ally tells Fish she's lost her first, ostensibly 'no-lose' case, it's Billy who supports her, but she barks at him too, leaving him puzzled (the first of many obtuse-Billy moments).

Billy's beautiful wife, Georgia, makes her entrance, and Ally greets her cordially, but burns inside. That night, Georgia visits her, saying Billy claimed he and Ally once 'had a few dates'.

Once Georgia and Ally confess that they hate each, they both feel better, and it's obvious that, however grudgingly, they like and admire each other.

The next day, Billy and Ally depose Billings, the harasser in Ally's former firm, who claims obsessive-compulsive disorder forces him to grab women.

The next morning, Fish himself meets with Billings, saying anyone creative enough to come up with the obsessive-compulsive disorder defence deserves a job offer. Ally is furious and threatens to quit, but Billings admits he made up the OCD claim and promises never to touch Ally again, at which point… Fish reveals

The office triangle: Billy (*Gil Bellows*) with the love of his life (*Calista Flockhart*) and the wife he loves (*Courtney Thorne-Smith*).

Calista Flockhart – stage and film actress, television lawyer and hotly debated pop cultural symbol.

At first, Billy Alan Thomas (*Gil Bellows*) told Georgia that he and Ally had only gone out on a 'few dates'.

Georgia Thomas (*Courtney Thorne-Smith*) has every reason to hate Ally, but she doesn't really. In fact, she and Ally share the same DNA – only it's Billy's.

Glenn (*Michael Easton*) and Ally: does size matter?

They've shared a courtroom and a bathroom, a slow dance and a bottle of wine. They've shared their songs, their dreams and their memories. They've even shared a therapist. What do you suppose the future will bring?

Courting controversy: Ally's clients have included a straying nun and a boy who wanted to sue God.

Vonda Shepard's album of music from the television series has sold nearly four million units worldwide. Not bad for a singer in a bar.

the offer was a ploy, and that he recorded the entire conversation for Ally's case.

Ally is angry at Billy because Billy told his wife that he and Ally only had a few dates. Back in Ally's office Georgia is waiting, angry because Ally told Billy that Georgia came to see her. Of course, they get it, at least temporarily, straightened out, and Billy does acknowledge that he was once desperately in love with Ally.

Ally doesn't want to meet with the Air National people because, she says, conference rooms make her feel small and juvenile. But during the meeting, though she's overcome by her memories and feelings of inadequacy, she manages to impress the National people and they decide to hire the firm.

Afterwards, they toast their success and Ally admits to Billy that she still loves him. He says he loves her too...as well as Georgia. Still later, Ally heads home alone, at the end of her stressful, but peculiarly rewarding, first week.

This pilot episode not only sounds the themes of many future *Allys*, and introduces Billy, Georgia, Renee, Elaine and the supremely self-satisfied Richard Fish, but the glamorous bar set, Vonda and her songs, and the ubiquitous Dancing Twins as well.

Generally, the critics lapped it up like a free martini.

Original Airdate: 8 September 1997

Compromising Positions

Ally McBeal is not only still in love with Billy Alan Thomas, but she's in love with the very idea of love itself...not to mention with truth-telling and fidelity, too.

Fish is in something approximating love too, with older women and, especially, with their drapey neck skin – that is, their wattles. And John Cage, the firm's other principal, whom we first meet in this episode, is not in love, though he'd quite obviously like to be, which is the proximate reason that he has – as the saying goes – 'consorted' with a prostitute, and as we meet him he's been busted for it. So Ally's second client at her new firm is the chastened Mr Cage, who sits in eloquent silence as the blithe Mr Fish explains the dilemma to the staff. Quite obviously, Mr Cage requires 'a moment' to recoup.

Cage's whore is not the only hooker paraded through this episode. Ally is distressed to learn that Billy did a little consorting himself on the occasion of his prenuptial bachelor party. And then Ally begins feeling rather like a prostitute herself when Fish asks her to go out with a prospective client, and it becomes clear that her legal expertise is not the primary attraction.

Ally and Billy draw the assignment to represent Cage at the hearing on the charge of soliciting a prostitute. At the hearing, Billy asks for a sidebar – a whispered conversation between the lawyers and the judge – and, to Ally's shock, the judge drops the charges against Cage. It turns out that Billy and the judge know each other.

In fact, Elaine explains later, the judge attended Billy's bachelor party, at which both Billy and the judge consorted. When Ally confronts Billy, he insists that going with the hooker was inconsequential, because, for men, there is a clear distinction between love and physical sex.

Ally goes out to dinner with Ronald Cheanie, the prospective client (played by Tate Donovan), Fish and his girlfriend, Jennifer 'Whipper' Cone, an older woman who turns out to be a judge. Ally is dismayed both by realizing that she's at dinner not in a professional capacity, but as a date, and also by seeing Cheanie kissing Whipper.

When she and Cheanie go off together for drinks, Ally realizes that he's a moral fellow after all and that she quite likes him, and they share a small kiss.

At the office the next morning, Fish pops out the bubbly to announce that Cheanie has signed. Ally tells Fish she saw Cheanie kissing Whipper, and Fish is devastated. Meanwhile, Billy wonders if he should confess to Georgia about the prostitute at the bachelor party.

Whipper tells Ally Cheanie's kiss was flattering, but meant nothing to her. Later, Cage argues to the office at large that hiring a prostitute was more noble than using another woman for meaningless sex. Everyone in the office applauds him except Ally.

When Billy starts to confess to Georgia, Ally interrupts and keeps him from telling. Ally and Georgia have lunch together, and to demonstrate the differences between men and women, Georgia turns and offers sex to a strange man. He immediately accepts. But when Ally tries it, the man turns out to be her brother's old room-mate.

Encouraged by Ally, who says she needs to believe that love and couplehood really work, Whipper makes up with Fish. That night, Ally dances with the Twins.

Original Airdate: 15 September 1997

The Kiss

The kiss is what Ally's thinking about as she prepares for her first official date with Ronald Cheanie by trying on a tight new pair of jeans. The kiss-off is what Ally's next case is all about: a fired TV anchorwoman (played by Kate Jackson, a former *Charlie's Angel*), who claims her wrongful termination amounted to sex-discrimination.

This is the episode that begins with what one TV critic called a 'lesbian sight gag', namely the shot of Elaine, her head at Ally's crotch level, helping Ally try on the new jeans. It's also the first of several times that we see the infamous blue-dumpster shot, the one not so subtly signifying rejection.

This is also the episode that explores the growing personal and professional bond between Ally and Georgia, who enlists Ally as co-counsel in the case of Barbara Cooker, the TV newswoman. As it happens, though, Georgia has a very good tactical reason for wanting Ally on the case as well: the attorney defending the station is the very same Jack Billings who sexually harassed Ally at her old firm.

The court case seems to be going well, and later the date seems to be going well too – Ally is flirtatious and charming and voluble – but the passionate and meaningful goodnight kiss that she so eagerly anticipates never materializes. Cheanie just gives her a peck on the cheek instead.

The next day in court a survey, commissioned by the TV station, purporting to show that men in the audience have no interest in sleeping with Cooker, is introduced. Billings gets Cooker to admit that age discrimination is an acceptable television-industry practice, and that she was fired because of her age, not her sex.

Cheanie keeps trying to talk to Ally, but she won't answer his calls, and when he shows up unannounced, Renee interrupts. The next day, Cheanie finally gets through to Ally and proceeds to break up with her. Billy comforts her, but Fish is only concerned that Cheanie doesn't break up with the firm too.

In court the battle continues, with Billings painting Cooker's suit as recrimination for a painful divorce and Ally getting Cooker's former boss, a station executive, to admit that Cooker's firing was a concession to stupid viewers and a compromise of his own integrity.

Georgia asks Ally to give their closing arguments and, emboldened, Ally asks Cheanie why he dumped her.

Ally is surprised to hear that Cheanie was afraid of falling for her and feared she would never be content in any relationship. Ally asks him to reconsider.

Later, Ally and Georgia agree that Elaine might be right about why they're so committed to Cooker's case: they're worried about getting older themselves.

In court, Ally tells the jury that they are the 'idiot' viewers of whom the television station executive was so dismissive, and she implores them to prove their intelligence by voting for Cooker. For his part, Billings argues that looks are a realistic factor in television. Later, he offers a settlement, which Cooker turns down. When the jury's verdict is announced Cooker is awarded damages – more than twice what Billings offered.

That night, Ally and Cheanie, and Georgia and Billy celebrate with a double date. For once, Ally's happiness is unalloyed. Meanwhile, Barbara Cooker, the victor, sits alone.

Original Airdate: 22 September 1997

The Affair

This is, in more than one way, a flashback episode. Not only does it concern the repercussions of an affair Ally once had with a professor who, in the present tense of the story, has just died, but the professor's widow is played with measured dignity by Kathy Baker, the female lead in *Picket Fences*, the first quirky and critically acclaimed David E. Kelley series.

More than that, this is the episode that introduces Elaine's deadpan wacky invention, the face bra.

While perky Elaine shows off her new invention, Fish tells Ally that John Dawson, their former law professor, has died and that Dawson's wife has asked for Ally to be one of the pallbearers. Not wanting to reveal the affair, Ally reluctantly agrees.

Flashbacks, to those school days, ensue. But Ally does reveal the affair, and confesses her guilty feelings, to Billy. When Katherine Dawson, the professor's widow, asks Ally – one of Dawson's favourite students – to speak at the funeral too, Ally feels compelled to agree.

In another flashback, Ally recalls how she finally broke up with the professor after she meeting his four-year-old daughter for the first time. That night, Ronald Cheanie, the firm's client whom Ally has been dating for nearly three entire episodes now, tells Ally her reliance on Billy, instead of him, is a concern: Why is she going to the wake with Billy and confiding in Billy, but not him?

At the wake, Ally looks down at Dawson in the open casket. Turning away, she finds Dawson's now eight-year-old daughter staring at her in a way that says she clearly remembers her, and that she knows the truth. The widow registers her daughter's reaction and, at that moment, realizes that Ally is the woman who almost broke up her marriage.

Later, Katherine Dawson confronts Ally, who doesn't deny the affair. Though we see in flashback Dawson's protestations of love for Ally, she tells his widow that it was merely his mid-life fling. Comforted to a degree, Katherine nonetheless tells Ally that she shouldn't speak at the funeral after all.

Cheanie isn't the only one bothered by Ally and Billy's confidences. Georgia tells Billy that it bothers her, too. Meanwhile, Cheanie confronts Ally, demanding to know about her and Billy, and Ally finally tells him about her affair with Dawson. This upsets Cheanie and he breaks up with her.

Later, at the funeral, the minister mistakenly calls for Ally to speak. Embarrassed, Ally at first blithers, but then she speaks about Dawson's devotion to his family. Katherine is moved. Afterwards, back in the office, Billy comforts Ally by taking her in his arms for a slow dance that promises more complications to come.

Original Airdate: 28 September 1997

One Hundred Tears Away

Here's the one about the crisps so good you can't keep your hands off them, even at the risk of disbarment and jail. It's not the last time our heroine will fall foul of the constabulary.

It's also the second episode in which a member of the Fish/Cage & Associates professional family ends up before the bar of justice. Which is to say this is the one that puts Ally herself on trial for being a little, shall we say, too tightly wrapped? Or, to put it more bluntly, for being annoying.

Between the press critics and the public concerns they ostensibly espouse, and the very best writers of series TV, there is a feedback loop. And David E. Kelley is certainly in the front rank of those writers, and he is certainly as savvy as they come.

The first wave of critical commentary about the new series was adoring, then came the inevitable backlash, and the second wave of criticism was of the Ally-is-a-privileged-whiner sort. So, with exemplary speed, scribe Kelley penned this episode to face those accusations head on, in a trial before an ominous Bar Association tribunal on Ally's emotional competence to practise law, no less.

In a late-night visit to a supermarket, Ally gets into a bitter argument with a woman over the last can of Pringles potato crisps on the store shelves. (The Pringles ad-campaign motto is 'Betcha can't eat just one.') The woman instantly despises Ally.

Cleverly, Kelley has the woman echo Ally's most severe social critics, calling Ally a 'pissy little thing' in Calvin Klein. When the woman ends up with the coveted last tube of Pringles, Ally, without thinking, trips her. She is summarily arrested.

When Renee bails Ally out, they learn shoplifting charges have been added to the assault claim, because a store security camera recorded Ally putting a tube of contraceptive jelly, into her pocket. Renee asks Ally why she was buying the jelly, but Ally won't say, and the next morning Billy represents Ally in court, where Renee is the prosecutor.

The judge grants a one-year continuance, with charges to be dropped if Ally stays clean. Back at the office, Elaine announces she has sold her 'face bra' invention and asks Ally to do the patent work, and Fish announces that the judge has reported Ally to the Bar Association and her licence to practise law has been suspended.

Judge Pink, an ally of Ally's old nemesis (and former harasser) Jack Billings, calls for a Bar Association hearing to investigate Ally's emotional stability, while back at the office Elaine reports she has been subpoenaed to testify.

That night, at their apartment, Renee is still curious about the contraceptive and about with whom Ally was planning to use it.

Ally says she was buying it as an expression of hope, in case someone like the Omar Sharif of *Funny Girl* was about to enter her life.

At the hearing the next day, the woman from the supermarket testifies about the fight, and later we learn that when Ally's erstwhile boyfriend Ronald Cheanie broke up with Ally and took his legal business elsewhere, he'd expressed some doubts about Ally's stability. Renee, too, has her doubts and she suggests Ally leave Cage/Fish if working with Billy is too stressful. But Ally, rather wanly, insists she's just fine.

When the hearing resumes, Elaine testifies that she once told someone that Ally seemed near a breakdown; that someone, Elaine tells Ally later, was Judge 'Whipper' Cone, Fish's girlfriend, who was then obliged to report Ally to the Bar Association panel.

Later, Ally takes the stand and, instead of defending herself, lashes out angrily at the inquisitorial panel. Afterwards, Billy, too, says he's curious about the contraceptive jelly, and Ally explains it rather winningly as a 'lottery ticket', in case her luck in love suddenly changes.

The next day at the hearing, Ally apologizes for her earlier outburst. Then Whipper appears and apologizes for reporting Ally, then defends her in a heartfelt speech, saying that when men are passionate, they are seen as strong, but when women are passionate, they are seen as being weak and emotional. Then Ally's friends – first Renee, then Billy – speak up for her, and for her emotions. Prudently, the board votes not to suspend Ally's licence and she and her friends celebrate at the bar. It isn't until she's walking home alone that Ally finally allows herself to cry.

Original Airdate: 20 October 1997

The Promise

Love for sale, sex as currency, the va-va-voom delivery girl and the hostile workplace and, of course, the obese love-struck attorney. This is the episode that offers just a hint that down that road there might be something between John Cage and Ally.

At the morning staff meeting, Ally gets two new cases: representing one of two ice cream stores embroiled in a trademark suit, and, with co-counsel John Cage, defending a high-priced call girl, who's herself a former lawyer (is there any other kind?).

When a beautiful young blonde delivery woman appears during the staff meeting, Fish and Billy ogle her with an obviousness (complete with special-effects tongues) that Ally and Elaine find offensive.

Later, at the courthouse, Harry Pippin, the opposing counsel and an obese apple of a man – whose method seems to be the filibuster, steamrolling right past all opposition – waddles in in mid-rant, successfully squelches one of Ally's motions and waddles out, still orating. In the hall, Ally has just barely introduced herself when Harry is felled by an apparent heart attack, and Ally has no choice but to perform mouth-to-mouth resuscitation – which we see from the stricken Pippin's point of view, Ally's face and lips in giant close-up. When Harry comes to, he's not merely grateful, he's in love.

Meanwhile, at the other hearing, at which Renee is the prosecutor, Cage/Fish's prostitute client recognizes John Cage as *her* former client. Afterwards, Ally visits the smitten Harry Pippin in the hospital and meets his fiancée, Angela, who also is overweight.

The next day, to Ally's surprise, Cage offers no cross-examination when a witness testifies that Sandra accepted money for sex. Later, Harry, out of the hospital, turns up to confess his lack of passion for Angela. He asks Ally if she could ever fall for him, but though she turns him down, she feels guilty, knowing her opinion of him is all about his weight. Given the real-world furore over Calista Flockhart's weight that was then underway, the moment is another clever fun-house-mirror refraction and commentary on the Great Anorexia Controversy.

Back in court, Cage, in one of his many peculiarly effective courtroom speeches against various letters of the law, argues that many women trade sex for money in one way or another, and that Sandra is just more honest about it. Later, Angela tells Ally she knows that Ally 'kissed' her fiancé – which is how Harry remembers the mouth-to-mouth – and asks Ally not to come to their wedding.

Later, Harry offers a settlement in the ice cream suit, which she accepts, and then asks for Ally's advice: should he marry Angela or wait for passion? Predictably, Ally votes for passion.

Later, Elaine complains to Billy that ogling the pretty, sexy young delivery woman is creating a 'hostile working environment' – which in the United States is the technical term for one of the two recognized types of sexual harassment in the workplace. (The other is 'quid pro quo', that is, demanding sexual favours in return for, say, a promotion or other favourable treatment. A hostile environment might result from pictures of naked women on wall calendars or a workplace tolerance for off-colour jokes or demeaning 'Baby'- and 'Sweetie'-type talk.) Elaine asks Billy to talk to Fish about the delivery woman incident, and later Billy does warn him that the firm could be facing a lawsuit.

In closing arguments in the prostitution case, Renee makes her familiar it's-the-law argument: Sandra broke the law, plain and simple. And Cage continues to argue that society permits women to exchange sex for money in many ways. It's an argument that annoys Ally, even though it's a winning argument with the jury, which finds Sandra not guilty.

Meanwhile, on the Pippin front, Ally learns from Angela that Harry has called off the wedding. Overweight people do not have the luxury of Ally's true-love romanticism, Angela says, and Ally realizes she has to get them back together. When Ally sees Harry, she convinces him that marriage is more about compassion than passion (an oddly poignant argument, coming as it does from arch-romantic Ally McBeal), and adds the clincher: who else other than Angela would ever date him?

The wedding is back on and Ally's invitation is reinstated. In a touching moment, Cage tells Ally not to lose her romantic ideals, even if the world is no longer a congenial place for romantics.

And at the wedding, Ally is still not certain that she did the right thing by bringing Angela and Harry back together.

Original Airdate: 27 October 1997

The Attitude

In addition to the vagaries of love and dating, this is the episode that has Georgia on its mind. It also introduces another John Cage peculiarity: like his real-life doppelgänger, he plays the bagpipes.

And while the world outside the TV show was already divided between those who found Ally to be admirable and those who did not, David Kelley – bravely? cleverly? – gives the detractors more ammunition in this episode, again highlighting Ally's short-comings, which, rather shockingly, include an almost wilful ignorance about the Jewish religion, as well as an overreaction to her latest date's rather meaningless dinner-table *faux pas*.

Billy's beautiful wife Georgia still does not work at Cage/Fish, but he will get her there through the expedient of a lawsuit. Georgia's boss, Jerry Burrows, is planning to move Georgia from litigation to the firm's corporate division, solely because his wife is jealous of her and doesn't want him and Georgia working together. Billy advises Georgia to talk to John Cage, who tells her to try to resolve the dispute herself once again before he acts on her behalf, but when she does Burrows won't rescind the transfer order.

Meanwhile, Renee has introduced Ally to Jason Roberts, a handsome prosecutor, who asks her to dinner, and Fish has assigned her to the case of Karen Horowitz (played by Brenda Vaccaro), who wants to sue her rabbi, because he won't grant her a Jewish divorce while her ex-husband languishes in a coma and can't give his consent.

When Ally meets with Rabbi Stern, she manages to insult him immediately with her casually dismissive gentile ways. She calls Jewish laws 'silly', and later refers to his yarmulka as a 'beanie', and, in an echo of the Pringles Lady, he reacts by calling her 'bitchy'. Stymied, Ally leaves in an angry huff.

Later, when Jason the handsome prosecutor visits the office, Ally, whose face is blotchy after Elaine's special acne treatment, tries to hide, thereby ironically counterpointing this episode's further example of her 'idealistic' intolerance of imperfection... in others: on their date, she's repulsed by the drops of salad dressing that land on the handsome prosecutor's chin, each one forever damning him in her memory.

Meanwhile, on the legal front: Karen's ex-husband dies, so she can now remarry, but the rabbi, still angered by Ally's attitude, has thrown Karen out of the synagogue and is refusing to perform her marriage service. And meeting with Georgia, cagey Cage merely announces that he's 'troubled', before leaving with the admonition that he will return. Georgia, understandably, is perplexed.

After Ally's date goes awry over Ally's obsession with the salad dressing on the prosecutor's chin, Renee tells her it's crazy to be so bothered, and that Ally will be alone forever if she doesn't change her ways.

Cage tells Georgia that her best option is either to accept her transfer or start looking for another job, but Georgia says she wants to sue for wrongful termination.

Ally's next meeting with the rabbi seems to be going no better than before, but this time he relents and offers to perform Karen's marriage and reinstate her in the flock. Of course, the rabbi, impressed by Ally's gentile gumption, is only angling for a date. Ally refuses.

Later, Renee admonishes Ally to stop dumping men on such flimsy excuses, so Ally decides to give the prosecutor, whom she kisses to erase the memory of the salad dressing, one more try. She even agrees to go out with the rabbi as part of her new policy of taking more chances with 'Mr Not Likelys'.

Meanwhile, the negotiations between Cage and Georgia's employer are moving forward (Cage prepares for them by playing bagpipes), and in his own low-key but devious way Cage wins a $311,000 settlement, payable immediately, for her. The only condition is that she will have to quit her job.

At which point Georgia get her 'temporary' position at Cage/Fish & Associates. Later, at the bar, everyone celebrates in the usual way – with glamorous lighting, Vonda Shepard music and dancing with the Dancing Twins.

Original Airdate: 3 November 1997

Drawing the Lines

Just in time for the all-important November Sweeps, one of three monthly periods when local ratings in the United States are exhaustively measured and advertising rates are set, the original sexual roundel that gave this series such erotic heat – Billy in uncomfortably close quarters with both his past and present loves – is set spinning once again.

What sets poor befuddled Billy's brain reeling is the sight of Ally instructing Georgia in the fine art of cappuccino-savouring, a scene that's not only comically erotic – with the orgasmic oohing and aahing and the close-ups of froth-stained lips – but, as almost everyone has not failed to notice, is more about the act of oral sex than sexual intercourse or, for that matter, coffee drinking.

After that bit of female bonding, closely and lecherously observed by both Billy and Richard, Georgia and Ally seem well on their way to becoming pals, and they certainly give every indication of being a good legal team when they're given the assignment of helping the wife of a rich man nullify her prenuptial agreement.

Ally, Fish, Cage, Billy and Georgia meet with the feuding Mrs Hatfield, who wants to divorce her wealthy husband without separating herself from his wealth. At the firm's first meeting with her, she (and we) become privy to one of Cage's less endearing idiosyncrasies: he rather blatantly picks his nose. But Mrs Hatfield does like the idea of having Ally and Georgia represent her, and it won't be the last time that a Cage/Fish client is hooked despite Messieurs Cage and Fish.

It's not a bitter, all-out war that Mrs Hatfield wants, but that's what she gets when Fish convinces her to investigate her husband. Later, when Fish gets photos of Mr Hatfield and another woman, Georgia and Ally are at first loath to use them; it's blackmail, after all. But they, do of course, and the photos promptly convince Mr Hatfield to negotiate a real deal.

Meanwhile, Fish and Billy are still ogling the delivery woman, so Elaine presents her complaint about the workplace, and her attorney, the rather blatantly named Caroline Poop (played by Sandra Bernhard), comes on the scene. She brings with her security-camera tapes of Billy and Fish caught leering and ogling, and reminds them that even if Elaine doesn't win, the lawsuit will be bad publicity for the firm.

Elaine tries to organize the firm's female employees to walk out, but it doesn't work: Ally gives her a talking-to that amounts to a dressing-down which cracks her easy-going shell and leaves her teary eyed; apparently her own attorney says they'll never win and Fish declares all he wants is for the firm to be a fun place to work. At any rate, the women refuse to walk out. Elaine demonstrates grace in defeat, saying it was important just to be heard, and Ally reassures a depressed Fish that the employees really do like the firm.

Meanwhile, Billy is overheated and disturbed by Ally's orgasmic cappuccino conversation, finally confessing to her that it reminded him of making love to her, and that he misses her.

Ally doesn't know what to say, so that night at home she cools her fevered confusion with ice cream. The next day at the office, Billy apologizes. Nonetheless, he brings more cappuccino too, but Ally tells Georgia she's through with the savouring ritual. At first, Ally and Billy agree to the need for boundaries if they are going to remain friends, but that night Ally tells him she's changed her mind: friends shouldn't have boundaries, even if it makes it more difficult. Billy agrees and they shake on it, and yet again Ally goes home alone.

Original Airdate: 10 November 1997

The Dirty Joke

It's fascinating, in this white-hot environment of series television, to watch as David E. Kelley plays with his viewers' pop-culture expectations as he orchestrates and interweaves his larger narrative themes.

This is the second Caroline Poop episode, and the lawyer is played again by actress–singer–comedienne Sandra Bernhard, the Mick Jagger look-alike and former Madonna pal who most viewers would surely know is widely assumed to be gay or bisexual. And this time Lady Caroline does file a sexual harassment suit against the firm – but not for Elaine; it's on behalf of the beautiful, bosomy delivery girl (Brooke Burns), who for this one episode briefly moves up from being set decoration and a plot point to an actual character, albeit minor.

This is also the duelling dirty jokes episode that not only satirizes Ally's otherworldly primness and propriety, but offers an opportunity for Vonda Shepard to move up too – from being just the throaty bar singer and bluesy piano player to actually delivering a line.

In fact, Ally is so prim-and-proper-seeming, such a Goody Two

Shoes incarnate, that she has merely to enter the unisex bathroom for Richard to instantly stop telling the gang his dirty joke.

Even Ally can see that her 'Julie Andrews demeanour' is putting people off. Sensibly, Renee suggests that Ally should tell an off-colour joke of her own, as a way of breaking the blue-stocking barrier between her and her colleagues. So Ally asks Renee to tell her a dirty joke, promising she won't be offended, but of course she's horrified by Renee's story of a headless, armless woman pitched into the sea by a man.

The next day, at the office, while Ally is discussing Renee's joke, the delivery girl appears, hands Fish an envelope and says she is suing the firm for sexual harassment. She contends that a 'hostile work environment' has been created – but, in a Kelley twist, it's not because of the leering men; it's caused by the women employees, who disapprove of her 'provocative' dress.

Later Ally, who still disapproves of Renee's joke, and Renee, who still insists it was funny, make a bet: Renee will tell the same joke in public, to the crowd at the bar, and if people laugh at her joke, Ally will have to get up on stage the next night and tell the one dirty joke she knows.

In the meantime, the Cage/Fish lawyers meet the delivery girl's attorney, the same Caroline Poop who'd represented Elaine in the abortive ogling lawsuit. Afterwards, Georgia declines Fish's request that she handle the firm's case, saying Caroline has given her provocative looks that she believes are sexual advances. That day, Caroline deposes Elaine, who denies any hostility toward the delivery girl, but still can't help commenting on the pretty blonde's 'slutty' dress and accusing her of 'flaunting' her ample bosom.

That night at the bar, Renee's joke kills. Everyone laughs. Even Ally can't help but smile. She concedes that Renee has won, and begs to be let out of the obligation to take her turn at stand-up comedy performance. But Renee insists: it's Ally's turn the next night.

The next day, Georgia catches Caroline giving her that peculiar look again, and later Georgia tells Billy she gets approached by gay women a lot, and also that Fish recently touched her neck.

The delivery girl tells Ally that it was Elaine's lawsuit that created the hostile atmosphere, and though Fish upbraids her for not questioning the delivery girl more thoroughly, Ally says that one answer was all she needed.

That night at the bar, Ally takes the stage to do her joke. And of course only Fish and Elaine laugh, but then Ally spots the rabbi – of all the people to be in the audience – with whom she's still scheduled to go out on a date. It is the depth of humiliation.

The next day, in court, Ally argues that if Elaine's lawsuit was the cause of the 'hostile environment', as the delivery girl testified, then there is no case, because lawsuits themselves are immune to such accusations. When the judge dismisses the case, Fish is thrilled with Ally. Back at the firm, the rabbi is waiting, and to her relief, he not only wasn't offended, it seems he's a connoisseur himself of off-colour humour. The rabbi even has a theory, a rather Talmudic one, of 'dirty' humour: According to the rabbi, a good dirty joke must have a victim and take advantage of someone's pain, which was precisely the case with Renee's joke.

When Caroline comes in to announce that now that the case is over the delivery girl will be returning to work, Georgia asks her just what those glances of hers mean.

Caroline replies she's just never seen a living Barbie doll before, which, to Georgia, is far worse than being taken for gay. Meanwhile, Billy confronts Fish about touching Georgia's neck and Fish promises it won't happen again. Then Fish calls the delivery girl aside and apologizes to her for the blatant ogling. His uncharacteristic sincerity is so moving to Ally that she gives him a kiss on the cheek.

Back at the bar later, Ally tells Billy that the great thing about dating the rabbi is that she knows from the start that it's not going anywhere and that it won't work out. Then, in a break from the weekly parade of Ally's episode-ending lonesome walks, those brave but melancholy hikes-with-musical-accompaniment down the mean streets of Boston, she and Renee walk home together, just two old pals out in the air, talking and joking.

Original Airdate: 17 November 1997

Boy to the World

This is the Christmas episode in which Vonda Shepard sings 'Jingle Bell Rock' and the Chipmunks' Christmas Song, Ally defends a teenage transvestite prostitute, Fish goes to court so he can mention his dead uncle's short-people prejudice in a eulogy and Cage labours under the misapprehension that he's dating Ally.

Critics generally thought this one of the best series episodes of the holiday season and one of the best *Ally*s yet.

Ally's interest in Jason, the handsome young prosecutor (of salad dressing fame) who is her current boyfriend, is paling, so she asks Renee to double date with them. Frisky Renee asks Ally to invite John Cage as her date. So, at the office, Ally asks Cage if he'll go out with her, Jason and Renee, and Cage accepts.

Meanwhile, Fish announces his short-people-hating uncle has died, but the minister won't allow him to mention the uncle's aversion in the eulogy. The minister maintains it isn't proper to celebrate 'bigotry' at a funeral.

Later, at court, Whipper Cone appoints Ally, who has her own phobia (she's afraid of criminals), as public defender for Stephanie/Steven, a beautiful young transvestite charged with prostitution. It's Stephanie's third arrest, Ally tells her/him, so conviction and jail time are almost certain.

That evening, Ally excuses herself early from the foursome when she gets an idea for Stephanie's defence. Arriving at Stephanie's apartment, she discovers that Stephanie has a real flair for clothing design, and she tells Stephanie they might be able to win their case if they plead that his transvestism fetish amounts to insanity. Stephanie doesn't want to be labelled insane – after all, it's what his family thought – but promises to consider it. The next day, Stephanie promises to make Ally a dress in lieu of her fee and also offers to do her make-up.

Meanwhile, Billy and Fish go to court to win the right for Fish to say what he pleases at his uncle's eulogy. They tell a judge the case has nothing to do with protecting the civil rights of short people, that instead it's about censorship and the right of free speech. Later, Whipper suggests to Fish that he might be using the lawsuit to avoid grieving for his uncle.

Back at the firm, Cage tells Ally he'd like to go out with her again, and Ally is shocked to realize Cage thought she was his date the night before.

That night, Ally brings Stephanie home to meet a psychiatrist, who says that Stephanie does indeed have a fetish, and some gender confusion, but knew what he was doing when he solicited a cop. After the doctor leaves, Stephanie applies Ally's make-up.

The next day, Cage is mortified by his mistake with Ally and she pleads Stephanie's case in court.

The judge postpones a verdict in the prostitution case for one year, on the condition that Stephanie gets a job and stays off the streets, and Ally herself agrees to hire Stephanie. Meanwhile, Billy and Fish plead their case to Judge Walworth (played by Armin Shimerman, Quark in *Star Trek Deep Space Nine*), who is short. But the judge hates political correctness and sees it as a pernicious kind of censorship, and he rules in their favour.

Meanwhile, Cage manages to ask Ally if she would ever really go out with him, and she says she might, but only if he wasn't her boss. It's an issue for Ally, but Cage, typically, continues to brood.

The next day, Fish delivers his uncle's eulogy, but doesn't mention short people. When he's done, though, the choir breaks into a gospel rendition of Randy Newman's 'Short People' song (the soloist is Jennifer Holliday, probably best known from *Dreamgirls*).

Back at the firm, Stephanie gives Ally the gift of a beautiful black dress and Ally tells Cage that she would like to have dinner with him some time. And that is where the typical, cloyingly sweet Christmas episode would end. But because it's David Kelley doing the plotting, this one continues.

That night, Ally and Renee are summoned to a crime scene. Stephanie has been murdered by a crazed customer. Cradling his body, Ally cries.

Later, Ally goes to the morgue and fixes Stephanie's wig and make-up, while Fish goes to the cemetery and bids his uncle goodbye.

Original Airdate: 1 December 1997

Silver Bells

This is Christmas episode number two, more traditional on the face of it, because it resorts to the hoary, hey-kids-let's-put-on-a-show device of a musical Christmas party at which the cast members, to some degree stepping out of the characters they play, show off their singing talents. This is also the episode about marriage, memory and threesomes.

Fish gives Ally the case of James, Mindy and Pattie – the Hortons – a threesome who would like to be legally married. Predictably, Ally is put off by the whole idea, and so is Judge Whipper Cone, who nonetheless agrees to hear the Hortons' testimony.

In court, James testifies that his marriage to Mindy was becoming dull until he met Pattie, and his new lover helped revive his relationship with Mindy too. Mindy says that it's nice to have a second mother around for the kids and that it's better not to have James sneaking around and having a double life. Later, Pattie testifies that she never expected to be in a polygamous relationship, but it makes having both a career and kids much easier.

Prompted by the Hortons' lifestyle, Georgia tells Billy that she realizes that since Ally came into their lives, he's been more open and intimate too. Billy denies it, but it's obviously true.

The Hortons' experience has stirred Cage's memory as well. He tells Ally he remembers that when his parents brought home his new brother he felt it was an intrusion at first, but grew to love the new baby.

When Fish rehearses 'I Love You More Today Than Yesterday', Elaine tells him Whipper would rather have a ring than a song. And later, while Elaine rehearses her back-up singers, Billy tells Ally what Georgia said about their relationship.

Ally says she never wanted to break them up, but doesn't want to be the best thing that ever happened to their marriage either. That night, Whipper and Fish discuss marriage. Fish asks her whether marriage is really all that important. She says it must be, because it scares him so much.

Later, Cage is too preoccupied pondering his feelings for Ally to help Fish work through his feelings about Whipper, and Georgia confronts Billy and Ally.

Georgia is angry – angry that Ally makes Billy a better person, angry that Ally makes her marriage to Billy stronger, angry that she even likes Ally. Faced with all this anger, Ally heads for court, where the 'sacred' institution of marriage is being debated. To the argument that the Hortons' arrangement trivializes the institution, Cage replies it isn't trivial to protect and honour the Hortons' loving home. That night, Judge Whipper visits the Hortons at home and finds more stability there than she had in either of her two marriages. (In real life Dyan Cannon did have a famously troubled marriage, to actor Cary Grant.)

The next day, Georgia convinces Billy that his close relationship with Ally amounts to less than total fidelity to her. Meanwhile, Cage prepares to ask Ally out again, pulling himself together, though he forgets to pull up his fly. Ally turns him down again.

As the Christmas party gets under way, the singing starts, with Elaine and her back-up singers doing 'I Saw Mommy Kissing Santa Claus'. Later, Renee and Vonda do 'Santa Claus Is Coming to Town' as a duet.

Fish is paged for the Horton verdict: Whipper rules that the polygamous marriage isn't legal, though it is successful. Later, Fish admits to her that he is afraid of marriage, saying that though he loves her, he doesn't want to turn out like his own parents, who fought all the time.

Meanwhile, Ally finds Cage alone in his office and says she'll go out with him after all. But this time, Cage declines. Down in the bar, Fish sings. Upstairs in the office, Ally and Cage share memories, a bottle of wine and a slow dance.

Original Airdate: 15 December 1997

Cro-Magnon

Does size matter? Do hallucinations matter? Is the tick-tick-ticking of her biological clock finally causing Ally to lose her grip on reality? This is the episode about the impressively endowed nude male model, the punch-out court case and the boxing match. It's also the episode in which Ally finally stops agonizing long enough to have a little crude fun. And of course this is the episode that introduces the Dancing Baby, arguably the most influential special effect since Captain Kirk first set the phaser on stun.

Ever in pursuit of personal improvement, Ally and Renee take a sculpture class, where they can't fail to notice that one of the nude male models appears to be extremely well-equipped. No sooner does Georgia hear about the model's extra-generous endowment than she decides that a little self-improvement might be in order for her as well, and she takes up sculpting too. Predictably, Billy disapproves.

Later, Fish introduces Ally to an important client, whose nineteen-year-old son, Clint, has been charged with assault because he punched out a would-be rival at a party. But Clint wants to avoid a guilty plea and the criminal record that would come with it, even though several people at the party are prepared to testify they saw him do it, so he wants a vigorous defence which Ally and Cage are to provide. Naturally, Ally finds herself physically attracted to Clint

– and it won't be the last time gamine-faced child/woman Ally will be attracted by a teenage boy/man.

That night, Ally is startled and disturbed by a recurring hallucination – an unearthly baby, dancing to, of all things, the song 'Hooked on a Feeling'. She even sees it in sculpture class!

In court the next day, Clint's victim says he didn't provoke the punch, but he does admit to calling Clint's date, who is his ex-girlfriend, a 'slut'. Ally tells the judge that if her chastity was impugned while out on a date, she certainly would want her boyfriend to stand up for her. Then, in an instant of imitating Cage, she says she's 'troubled' and takes a 'moment' for a time-out.

Later, while Ally is with Renee at a coffee shop, the art-class model, Glenn, who is no hallucination, appears and asks Ally out.

Meanwhile Billy, who's heard all about the well-endowed male model, asks the women if 'size' really does matter. Of course they all say no, but Billy still has his doubts.

Cage too has heard about the penile-advantaged male model, and furthermore knows that Ally is going to go out with him, but prudently he declines to know more details, suggesting only that Ally might want to call an anthropologist as a witness in Clint's case.

That night, Ally tells Renee about her hallucinations, and Renee, good rationalist that she is, says the dancing baby must be a symbolic materialization of Ally's ticking biological clock.

The following day, the firm's men, good Cro-Magnons in nice suits all, start an office betting pool on a big upcoming boxing match, to which Billy is dragging an unwilling Georgia. Billy's sensitive-guy manhood is still troubled by the 'size' issue and he questions Georgia about her satisfaction in bed – if she ever wishes he was 'bigger'. Of course Georgia reassures him.

At Clint's trial, Cage's Zen approach to litigation is demonstrated yet again when he calls the anthropologist to the stand, then dismisses him without a single question.

That night, Ally has drinks with Glenn, who turns out to be a professional snowboarder with the requisitely casual approach to the big issues in life – the diametric opposite of the jaw-clenchingly obsessive Ally McBeal. Still, later Ally confides to Renee that she would have gone to bed with Glenn in an instant, had he only asked.

Meanwhile, Billy's own obsessing – over the burning does-size-matter question – has left him temporarily impotent, unable for the first time ever with Georgia. She takes it as a compliment, however, thinking his paralyzing need to impress her is wonderfully sweet.

In court the next day, Cage – not for the last time – appeals quietly to the jury's emotions by recounting a story from his own life – this time when he didn't stand up to a bully and was haunted by his failure to act for years. He felt like a man for the first time years later, he says, only after he actually did punch another bully.

Which is to say, for anyone who might have missed it, that even meek and deliberate John Cage says he only felt like a man by acting like a caveman; in other words, like the Cro-Magnon of this episode's title.

Meanwhile, Ally arranges a second date with Glenn, Georgia still can't get out of her arrangement to go with Billy and the guys to the prize fight, and Fish tells Ally he once rid himself of a similar apparition by giving in to it.

Back in court, the jury acquits Clint. Ally gives him a big victory hug, but in a moment of what's good for the Cro-Magnon goose is good for the Cro-Magnon gander, she can't resist giving his teenage backside a good squeeze as she does.

Then, in a scene nicely intercut between the boxing match and Ally's date, as Georgia and the men watch the fight, Ally and Glenn go back to her apartment, plunk out a little 'Heart and Soul' on the piano, kiss and, as the big fight heats up, make passionate love on the floor.

Later, with Glenn gone, Ally rejoices in her new-found knack for having a simple and satisfying one-night stand. Then, in her adorably oversized PJs, she spots the baby again and has a nice dance with it.

Original Airdate: 5 January 1998

The Blame Game

The shoe is on the other foot in this episode about the varieties of liability. The pants are down around the ankles as well. Yes, it's the Penguin episode.

Blame Game Number One is of the deadly serious variety: Ally, Cage and Georgia try a case about liability in an aeroplane crash. Blame Game Number Two begins while Ally and Georgia are sipping their cappuccinos at the local Starbucks, that upscale, Seattle-based coffee-house company that first appeared on every intersection in every city of the United States and now seems well on its way to conquering the world. There they run into well-endowed nude male model Glenn, Ally's recent one-night stand, who's supposed to be out of the country, and who later proceeds to make her feel guilty about using him as a sexual object, saying that was why he never called after their first date. To prove that's not true, Ally agrees to go out with him again.

At the office, Ally, Cage and Georgia discuss how to prove liability against the airline involved in the crash that killed the father of the Lamb family, which they're representing.

In court, their first ploy backfires: their expert witness, who contends that mechanical failure was the most likely cause of the plane crash, is quickly discredited because he's also a believer in alien abductions.

That night, Ally again has sex with Glenn. Only, unlike the previous encounter, this time we don't get to see it. But we do hear about it afterwards, when Ally meets her friends at the bar and they all know where she's been and what she's been doing.

The next day, Glenn asks Ally to dinner, and Ally confesses to Renee that she's really starting to like him, even though they have absolutely zero in common. But surprisingly, that night Glenn maintains that Ally still sees him as a sexual object and he breaks up with her, which leads Ally to realize that Glenn manipulated her into sex the second time, and that he no more intended to actually have a relationship than she did. So she and Renee plot an old revenge scam with a catchy new name: the Penguin.

Meanwhile, the airline-liability case is bringing the firm attention from the TV news, and with it comes additional pressure to win. In a settlement conference, Ally, reasoning very much like Cage, contends that, whether or not the airline was actually negligent, a jury will assume that planes don't just fall from the sky without someone somewhere making some sort of mistake, and that the jurors will vote to place blame. The airline offers the Lambs $375,000 to settle, but the lawyers disagree as to whether or not the family should take it: Georgia, Ally and Cage think it's a good amount, but Fish says they should hold out for better.

Later, Billy scolds Ally about being 'promiscuous' with Glenn, citing the damage it could do to her professional reputation. Ally says Billy has no right to comment on who she dates and shouldn't try to hide his jealousy behind 'professional' concerns.

Back in court, Cage makes his closing arguments, urging the jury to 'spank' the airline into safety consciousness with a large cash penalty.

That night, Renee flirts with Glenn in sculpture class. Later, driving down a lonely street with him, Renee has no trouble convincing Glenn to pull over, get out of the car and drop his pants. Ally and Georgia watch through binoculars as Renee backs away, enticing Glenn to pursue her. He waddles after her like a penguin. When Ally and Georgia drive by, Renee jumps in the car, and they leave Glenn penguin-walking after them.

The next morning in court, the case goes to the jury. While Fish frets over the pending verdict, Ally finds Glenn and Billy back at the firm and she apologizes to both of them, saying that when someone gets hurt the natural tendency is to cast about for someone to blame, and that's what she did.

Back at court, the airline offers one last settlement, almost doubling their first offer. The lawyers recommend that the family take it, but the Lambs have grown lion-hearted and refuse. Now Fish is more worried than ever, but then the jury finds for the family and awards them one million dollars. Everyone celebrates at the bar, including Ally, who seems happy for once.

But in the world outside the show, the fact that the only man Ally has yet had sex with turns out to be nothing more than a male bimbo whose best characteristic is his large member, combined with the petty and childish trick she perpetrates to get her revenge, gave the critics of Ally-as-role-model more ammunition and the series that much more publicity.

Original Airdate: 19 January 1998

Body Language

More than half-way through the first season of the pop-culture TV sensation of the year, and with an entire other series (*The Practice*) to write, David E. Kelley finally brings in co-writers for the first time. The result is the episode about the battling bridesmaids, the sperm-donating convict and Fish's improbable pick-up of Attorney General Janet Reno, the highest law-enforcement official in the United States, in a bar. As if that wasn't enough, it's also the episode thast finds hapless John Cage attempting smile therapy.

Kelley's co-writers for this meditation on marriage are Dawn Prestwich and Nicole Yorkin, who also lends her last name to one of the episode's minor characters, Prison Superintendent Yorkin.

At a wedding in which they're both bridesmaids, condemned to wear the requisite hideous dresses, Ally, in a demonstration of aggression that would do a hockey player proud, beats out Renee and the rest of the competition to snag the bouquet. Afterwards, she and Renee burn their dresses and vow never to be bridesmaids again.

By comparison, the bouquet-toss scene was also done a season later on the sublimely satirical *Sex and the City* cable series, about four young and sophisticated single women in Manhattan. As the bouquet arced through the air above them, the four women, drinks and cigarettes in hand, eyed it appraisingly as it soared through the air and fell…at their feet. Then, without missing a beat or paying the fallen flowers any attention at all, they muttered their goodbyes and departed the reception.

Later, in court, Ally and Georgia team up to try to convince a judge that Michael, a mad-bomber prison inmate with a life sentence, should be allowed to marry Janie, his fiancée. The judge rules that it's Prison Superintendent Yorkin's decision to make. When Georgia and Ally meet with him, Superintendent Yorkin says inmates are allowed to marry only if they have children, and that no conjugal visits between unmarried people are permitted for the purposes of making children.

Back at the firm, Cage is up to something fishy – smile therapy – while Fish is his usual cagey self at the bar, where he spots the Attorney General of the United States, a tall, no-nonsense older woman who wears no-nonsense glasses, who just happens to be the woman of his dreams.

Whipper sees Fish flirting with the AG, touching the wattles on her neck and so forth, and she breaks up with him. The next day, Fish is neither happy nor, despite Cage's best therapeutic efforts, can he summon up a smile. He tells Cage he doesn't think he can get back together with Whipper without resolving the marriage issue, something he's not prepared to do, so Cage shows Fish how smile therapy works: look into a mirror, smile, visualize an outcome, then go after it.

Ally's not above trying out a little smile therapy herself on behalf of a client, so she flirts with the judge in the matrimony-minded convict case. When this doesn't work, she sprouts the seed of an ingenious plan: Janie can be artificially inseminated with Michael's sperm and conceive a child that way! And then Superintendent Yorkin will have to allow them to get married!

Meanwhile, Fish tries to make up with Whipper, complimenting her beauty. Her response – apropos the subject of insemination – is to knee him in the groin.

Presently, everyone has agreed to Ally's insemination plan, and soon she and Georgia are back at the prison, with a plastic cup and sexy magazine for the superintendent to pass on to Michael. Soon after, Ally and Georgia are racing with the filled cup to Janie, who is awaiting them at a fertility clinic. But inevitably, they're pulled over by two cops, a male and a female, who demand to see what's in the cup. The male cop is clueless, but the policewoman takes one look and knows.

Sent on their way again, Ally and Georgia arrive at the clinic only to find Janie has changed her mind about the insemination, but then, providentially, Superintendent Yorkin, perhaps having by now succumbed to smile therapy, changes his mind, permitting Janie and Michael to marry after all. And despite her recent vow, when Janie asks Ally to be a bridesmaid she finds that she can't refuse.

Meanwhile, Fish offers Whipper an apology and a qualified commitment; they make-up and kiss, and that's when she discovers that he's prudently put on a protective athletic cup.

Later, at the prison, a minister marries Janie and Michael, who in an aside to Ally and Georgia tells them that his inspiration for the sperm donation was his vision of them – together. Still later, Ally dances out on the street in the falling snow, in her pyjamas no less, while her friends watch smiling. Cute, pleasing to watch, but – even in the whimsical universe of the show – more than a little improbable.

Original Airdate: 2 February 1998

Once in a Lifetime

David E. Kelley shares original-story credit (with Jeff Pinkner), though he wrote the teleplay himself, for this episode about undying love and the memorably disastrous first date between Ally and John Cage, during which the far-too-overwrought Cage far-too-zealously seizes a moment, which he subsequently suspects was, just perhaps, somewhat 'untoward'. Billy may be

Ally's soulmate, but – as Ally has yet to discover – it's she and John who are most alike.

The day before her long-awaited first date with Cage, Ally realizes she really doesn't want to go out with him after all and avoids him before the morning meeting, at which Fish assigns her to represent a famous elderly artist whose adult son and guardian refuses to let him marry his much younger, twentysomething fiancée. But the crusty, white-haired old artist (played by Richard Kiley) wants a man for an attorney, not a little girl in a little miniskirt, so Fish teams Ally with Billy on this case that turns out to be all about undying true love.

But it's not the artist's love for the young Paula, his fiancée, explains the son, Sam. Instead, the artist is still in love with his first, dead wife, whom he paints – obsessively – and with whom he still holds conversations, in which the dead woman offers him advice. The artist admits all this, but says he loves Paula too. Ally and Billy do not believe him.

Cage, meanwhile, has begun obsessing over whether or not to kiss Ally on their date. Fish's advice: women like aggressive men. Then Cage tells Fish he fears he's a poor kisser with too much saliva. Fish suggests consulting Billy on how Ally likes to be kissed, but Billy is very uncomfortable with the entire subject.

Back in court, we learn that the artist once bought a very expensive boat, ostensibly at his dead wife's request. Paula declines Sam's offer of all his father's money not to marry. It proves she is not after money, but confounds everyone about her true motives. If she's not after his money then what does she want? Ally and Billy wonder, and, as they reminisce about their own once-in-a-lifetime love, Ally fantasizes that Billy gives her a passionate kiss.

Back in court, the artist is on the witness stand, questioned by Ally, who's doing well until he begins talking on the stand to the dead woman, suggesting that Sam might have been right all along.

Afterwards, Paula admits she only wants to marry the old man so she can become his guardian and open a gallery to sell paintings of his dead wife, which Sam won't let him do. Sam shows Billy and

Ally the paintings in question. They're good, but not up to the standards of his earlier work, and Sam says he fears they will ruin his father's artistic reputation if they're offered to the public.

Meanwhile, Cage has been getting kissing tips from Elaine, building up his courage and rehearsing his moves for his date with Ally by listening to the deep-voiced, sexy seventies-era soul music of Barry White (best known for such heavy-breathing, pulse-pounding numbers as 'Can't Get Enough of Your Love, Babe' and 'You're the First, the Last, My Everything', and who, incidentally, rode his *Ally McBeal* exposure to a come-back of sorts, which led to a new album, *Staying Power*, and a multi-city tour with Earth, Wind & Fire in the late summer of 1999. But that tour had to be postponed when the veteran soul-pop singer suffered nervous exhaustion. He was also hospitalized for hypertension during a 1995 tour in support of a previous new album).

At any rate, thus buoyed, Cage takes Ally out for their date. But Ally goes overdrive into full-on dumping mode, chattering non-stop through the entire evening about clothes, make-up and other subjects designed to drive anyone in earshot to distraction. Finally, back at the door to her door, Cage lunges at Ally with a kiss that literally knocks her to the ground before she escapes into the safety of her apartment.

The next morning, Ally literally runs into Cage and tells him she has no interest in dating him, which he interprets as meaning she's still in love with someone else, who is probably still in love with her too.

In court, Ally makes the not-unexpected argument that everyone should be so lucky as to experience a love that will not die, and the judge rules that the artist will be able to open his gallery to sell his paintings of his dead wife.

That night, in a final montage over music that speaks volumes without saying a word, Georgia and the distracted Billy are dancing, the lonely artist is gazing at the paintings of his late wife, Cage is adjusting to being dumped and Ally is walking home alone.

Original Airdate: 23 February 1998

Forbidden Fruits

Married people, whether Billy or the client's new wife, are the fruits forbidden in this latest episode about the vagaries of marriage and the rocky course of true love, featuring an exasperated Georgia steeling herself and finally telling Ally and Billy to just get it over with and...go ahead and do it!

The firm represents United States Senator James Foote, who is accused of breaking up his new wife's former marriage. The problem is not just Anna Flint, the well-named opposing counsel, who has a reputation for sweet-talking juries while scorching the opposition, but the fact that Fish himself has decided to lead the charge on this one. And that gives David Kelley the opportunity to deliver a prescient opinion about a recent real-world legal ruling.

At the hearing, Fish argues that Senator Foote's case should be postponed because it will interfere with his ability to do his job, and he even cites the Supreme Court's then-recent ruling in the President Clinton versus Paula Jones case – that a politician can be sued while in office – calling it a 'screw-up', but the judge doesn't buy the ploy.

Afterwards, Counsel Flint, speaking for approximately half a stirred-up nation then debating the workplace propriety of Ally's miniskirts, tells Ally bluntly that her skirt is too short.

In court the senator's wife's ex-husband testifies that their marriage was happy until the senator began his avid pursuit, while Ally argues that two people who fall in love cannot be blamed for it, and adds somewhat incongruously that just admitting their feelings isn't necessarily an adulterous act.

In fact, the case has set Ally to wondering about propriety herself, and just what her position really should be on people who break up other people's marriages. Meanwhile, Georgia hasn't been able to help noting the familiarity of the courthouse argument, and she confronts Billy and Ally, and then walks off the case.

Back in court, the question is just how avidly did the senator pursue the woman who was then another man's wife, and Cage offers the ingenious argument that anyone might be so moved by a piece of music that he would invite someone to dance, and he illustrates this by putting on some music and dancing with Ally.

That night, Renee, ever the practical rationalist, suggests that Ally might try therapy for dealing with her feelings for Billy, but Ally says she prefers 'being a mess'.

Later, when Billy tells Ally he and Georgia are seeing a therapist, who wants to talk to her too, Ally refuses.

Fed up, Georgia gets mad and suggests Ally and Billy just get together for a night to get 'it' out of their systems. Billy tries to assuage Georgia's anger by telling her that the fact that he once loved Ally only makes it easier for him to recognize the stronger love he has for her.

The next day, at the office, Georgia apologizes to Ally, and Elaine suggests to Georgia that she should have an affair, to make Billy realize how much he's risking.

Back in court, Ally argues that if two people really love each other, they'll end up together, and that the senator's current marriage is the sacred one. Quite sensibly, Billy tells Georgia he feels the same way about their marriage. The judge rules in favour of the senator, and Georgia rules in favour of Billy, and both the senator and Billy thank Ally. Naturally, everyone celebrates. But Ally still hasn't quite abandoned the idea that first love might turn out to be the best love in the end.

Original Airdate: 2 March 1998

Theme of Life

Do you have a theme song? John Cage does, and his therapist thinks Ally should too.

Forget the stormy debate that up till now has accompanied this show. Any series graced with a recurring cameo by Tracey Ullman as the snippy therapist is most likely squarely on the side of the angels, and hip beside. (It's a sentiment that the members of the American Academy of Television Arts and Sciences apparently share, naming her Best Guest Actress in a Comedy at the 1999 Emmy Awards.)

Not only does Ally get her own theme song in this episode, but she gets a new love interest, in the person of Dr Greg Butters (Jesse L. Martin), as well as the opportunity to have an actual knock-down-drag-out fight with Georgia in their kick-boxing class. It won't be the last time Ally and Georgia tangle.

In the world outside the show, Calista, faced with censure and condemnation over her scrawny, yet muscled arms after she had the temerity to wear yet another sleeveless dress to yet another awards show, defended herself by pointing out she'd been taking kick-boxing lessons. At the bar of public morality then, this episode's Ally–Georgia fight scene is Exhibit Number One.

Ally is preparing for a trial in which she is defending Dr Greg Butters, an attractive young surgeon accused of transplanting a pig's liver into a woman without her permission. Oddly enough, though the woman is given a name, Hanna Goldstein, that the audience might assume was Jewish, nothing is made of her possible religious objections to the transplant. Instead, she just objects to having her life saved by a 'big fat hog'.

When Ally walks Dr Butters to his car, he is clearly attracted to her, but she is distracted by another visitation from the Dancing Baby. Moreover, on her way home, she spots Fish and Janet Reno giggling together as they dash into a nearby apartment building. Ally tells Georgia and Billy about seeing Fish and the Attorney General.

When Whipper finds out, she confronts Janet Reno, who denies Fish ever propositioned her and calls Whipper a 'bitch' for interfering. The next morning, Fish pleads with Whipper to forgive him and take him back, but she says it's over for good.

It's not surprising that, to deal with her stress, Ally has taken up kick-boxing, along with Renee and Georgia. Noticing Ally's limp after a workout, Cage recommends she see his smile therapist instead of exercising, but Ally declines. Later, at a workout, the trainer assigns Ally and Georgia to fight each other in a match the next day.

Meanwhile, Billy suggests that Fish may be fooling around with Reno because he's running away from his true feelings for Whipper.

Back in court, Dr Butters testifies that the hog liver was the best option for Hanna, but under cross-examination admits he would have lost a major grant if he hadn't performed the procedure by the end of the year. Ally is furious with Butters for not telling her this little detail.

Later, after more visions of the Dancing Baby and the disturbing hallucination of swimming through an underwater version of her world, Ally finally sees Cage's blunt-talking therapist, Dr Tracy Clark, whose advice about the proposed kick-boxing fight is to 'Smack her!' and who tells Ally that what she really needs is a good theme song. (Ally's pick is 'Tell Him'.)

That night, everyone gathers at the gym for the big kick-boxing grudge match. Ally and Georgia square off, tentatively at first, then more aggressively, each landing major blows as their friends, especially Billy, watch uncomfortably. The match ends in a double knockdown tie, and afterwards Ally and Georgia feel better about each other.

In court, Butters has rejected a settlement. And on her way there for closing arguments later, Ally hums her theme song. She even begins dancing a bit to it. It's so darn catchy, in fact, that the whole street-corner crowd begins to dance to the tune with her.

At the trial, Cage closes by telling the jury that Dr Butters saved Hanna's life with the transplant, which is all that counts. Later, while they are waiting for the verdict to come in, Elaine comforts Fish on his break-up with Whipper and, because she's the firm's girl who can't say no (as no less an authority than Jane Krakowski has described the character), offers him physical comfort if he wants it.

Of course, the verdict comes in for Dr Butters, and he proposes dinner with Ally, who, still attracted, accepts. As he gives her a small kiss in the courtroom, Whipper watches wistfully. Then Ally and Georgia, two bruised boxing buddies, head off together for a beer.

Original Airdate: 9 March 1998

The Playing Field

The attorneys of Cage/Fish are out there on the playing field alright...way out there. Whether it's courtship or the courthouse, in this episode the games and surreal antics David E. Kelley choreographs for them seem both increasingly private and increasingly fantastic. Which is to say, would you want an attorney who argues, as Fish does, that disgruntled lesbians were the driving force behind sexual harassment laws? For that matter, would you want an attorney who's a nine-year-old boy?

In an arch reference to *Doogie Howser, MD*, the show about a teenage doctor he produced and wrote, David E. Kelley conjures up a courtroom opponent for Ally in this episode who's a little boy, a child prodigy given to sulks and tears. Do his tantrums level the playing field, much like the sexual harassment laws level the playing field for women in a man's world?

Ally has another session with her new therapist, Dr Tracy Clark (Tracey Ullman), who calls Ally a 'weakling' for her reliance on romances and men, and she encourages Ally to deal forcefully with her fantasies, by kicking the Dancing Baby in the bottom and walking through the water whenever she feels she is drowning.

Meanwhile, Dr Greg gives Ally a ride to work, and on the way, looking at Ally instead of the road, he runs through a stop sign and collides with another car. Ally's lawyering instincts take over and she suggests that both drivers exchange insurance information and not admit liability.

Later, Fish, Billy and Georgia meet with Eva Curry, who claims she was the victim of sexual harassment because she decided not to climb the corporate ladder by having sex with Mr Tyler, her boss, and her career suffered as a result. In court, however, Curry admits she never met Tyler and has never been harassed by him in any way. But the women who did have sex with Tyler all received promotions. The judge rules in favour of the case proceeding.

The next morning, Ally thinks she sees the Dancing Baby, and following Dr Clark's suggestion, she gives it a good kick. But the fantasy baby turns out to be a real child, who turns out to be Oren Koolie (played by Josh Evans), the other driver's attorney, a nine-year-old prodigy who looks even younger than his nine years. Once Oren stops crying, his budding legal instincts assert themselves, and he asks for $125,000 in damages.

Meanwhile, Renee has suggested that Ally find her self-esteem on her own body (Renee's not surprisingly is in her breasts). Ally picks her lips, which she feels are the most attractive part of her body next to her eyes. Later, while Greg grows uncomfortable, Ally fantasizes that her lips grow into a huge pucker.

Ally, who seems to need it, returns to Dr Clark for more therapy, and Clark tells her that Dr Greg is afraid of her because he knows she is the right woman for him, which Ally finds hard to believe.

When Ally again meets with Oren, she offers no settlement, and Oren dissolves into tears. Later, Ally sits Oren in her lap and reminds him that he is still just a child. Oren, snuggling, begins negotiating. Later, Oren disappears under the table when Ally refuses to agree to his settlement terms.

In court, Fish makes one of his provocative and non-politically correct arguments, saying that lesbians were the driving force behind sexual harassment laws, and that women should qualify under the Federal Disabilities Act, because they cannot cope with office romances. The judge rules the 'preposterous' harassment claim must nonetheless proceed to trial.

Later, Oren wonders aloud who made up the rule that it's a man's world, and Ally and Oren settle the auto-accident claim for $35,000.

Fish, who in the world outside the show is widely taken to be the closest to David Kelley's alter ego among the characters, turns up and gets a tongue-lashing from Ally and Georgia, who are offended by his courtroom antics, but predictably the scolding only arouses him.

Later, Dr Clark encourages Ally to use her sex appeal as power, and when Ally informs Dr Greg that she settled his case, she moves closer to him, quite clearly offering her self-esteem-sensitive lips. Greg insists he has never kissed a girl he hasn't danced with first, so Ally takes his hand and the pair dance.

Original Airdate: 16 March 1998

Happy Birthday, Baby

At your last birthday, did all your close friends hop up to perform show-stopping tunes for you? No? Perhaps that's because your friends aren't Broadway pros masquerading as lawyers and doctors (and a secretary). Ally doesn't like being reminded that she's turning another year older – and still single – any more than Calista likes talking about her age in the world outside the show.

This is the episode in which Ally turns twenty-eight, the firm represents a courtly foot fetishist and Dr Greg announces he's taking a hospital job in Chicago (perhaps on David Kelley's other show). And Kelley continues to tweak viewers' expectations about race and romance by continuing to ignore the issue.

Dr Greg Butters gives Ally an end-of-the-evening kiss, but passes up her invitation to come upstairs, frustrating her mightily, so she takes it out on her plastic inflatable guy doll. Ally's not a fetishist, it's just that she's about to turn twenty-eight and she needs some comfort – but the firm's newest client is.

Mark Henderson is being prosecuted (by Renee) for sneaking into Cheryl Bonner's flat in the middle of the night and tickling her feet. In court, Cheryl describes how she awoke, saw Mark, began screaming and called the police.

Cross-examining her, Ally establishes that Henderson and Bonner were dating at the time, and that the door to Bonner's apartment was unlocked when Henderson came in. When Ally and Renee discuss the case later, Ally gives Renee an orgasmically pleasurable foot massage, while Cage and Fish listen at the door.

Back at the trial, Henderson explains that when Cheryl expressed a love for erotic foot massages, he simply decided to surprise her. Later, after he's described his adoring foot caresses, Henderson surprises Ally by refusing to allow an insanity plea.

Elaine, playing the musical impresario again, invites Dr Greg to sing at Ally's surprise birthday party, and of course he's got a sexy, stage-worthy voice that makes every woman in earshot swoon.

Ally has brought Mark and Cheryl to the bar, trying to affect a reconciliation outside the spotlight of the trial. But, to her embarrassment, the bar's spotlight hits her, and the musical birthday interlude gets under way. First Vonda, then Elaine, then Renee sing 'I'm a Woman', then Greg and Renee sing a sizzling 'Don't' duet that sets Ally jealously wondering if they just might.

Back at the apartment, Renee is insisting she has no interest in Greg, when Dr Greg himself drops by and drops the bombshell that he's leaving Boston to take position at a Chicago hospital. Then he drops the real bombshell: If things had worked out differently, he says, he could have fallen in love with her.

Ally affects an impassive unconcern, but later she sits on the inflatable doll until it explodes.

Meanwhile, Mark has overheard Cheryl telling Ally that, until his 'sick' behaviour, she'd thought Mark just might turn out to be Mr Right, and he's apologized for his untoward behaviour. Later, in court, Ally argues that the issue isn't feet, it's going into a person's home without being invited, and she blames Mark's act on loneliness, not insanity.

Back at the office, the staff surprises Ally with a birthday party. When a male stripper dressed as a cop breaks into a bump and grind, everyone, except Elaine, leaves the room.

The jury finds Mark Henderson not guilty, and then he and Cheryl arrange to meet for coffee.

Original Airdate: 6 April 1998

The Inmates

The inmates aren't running the asylum by themselves in this episode – a murder case (and the imminent May Sweeps) requires Cage/Fish to bring in Donnell & Associates, David Kelley's other televised legal team, while Renee's frisky boldness with a man lands her on the other side of the dock, as a defendant in an assault case.

And Fish, who even manages to get in a little wattle-stroking, bangs away oratorically at the sex discrimination laws again, representing a trendy restaurant that fired a waiter because he was not gay.

Ally, who pleads that she prefers her cases more soft core, faints dead away at the scene of an axe murder and is horrified that the firm's client is the dead man's wealthy wife, Marie Hanson, who has been arrested for the axe murder. Marie explains that she doesn't remember the killing, that she experiences black-outs and that her psychiatrist had prescribed medication.

Meanwhile, when Fish and Georgia meet with the lawyer representing the waiter who claims he was fired from a French bistro because he's heterosexual, Fish makes the argument that it's perfectly acceptable to fire someone based on their sexual orientation.

'You need somebody fey to move the crème brulée,' he says blithely, shocking Georgia as much as the opposing attorney. Later, in court, Georgia is arguing that there's no special protection for heterosexuals, when Fish interrupts to argue the client was dismissed because he could not perform a 'function of the job', which was meeting the expectations of the restaurant clients that they could expect good gay waiters with good gay panache, whose presence would make them feel sophisticated. Afterwards, Georgia tells Fish in no uncertain terms that she will no longer be associated with his bigotry. Back in court, however, the judge urges the restaurant's attorney to work out a deal, saying that there are a 'lot of people like Richard Fish out there'.

Meanwhile, Fish brings the tough, no-nonsense Donnell & Associates lawyers in on the axe-murder case, and at a meeting Bobby Donnell (Dylan McDermott) is simply agog at the goings-on around Cage/Fish, while Ally – at her most blithering, pratfalling and fantasizing – is simply agog over him.

Outside the world of the show, in the on-going trial of Ally-as-role-model in the court of public opinion, it's Ally in this episode, at her most incompetent and moonstruck, that's Exhibit A.

Later, Ally and Bobby meet with Marie Hanson's psychiatrist, who tells them she may suffer from a neurological disorder, and may have committed the murder during a black-out.

The psychiatrist is reluctant to testify, however, fearing it could harm his practice and his credibility if it becomes public knowledge that, while under hypnosis, Marie Hanson assumed the identity of Lizzie Borden, and moreover seemed to know little-known details about the infamous axe murder's life.

Meanwhile, relations between Cage/Fish and Donnell & Associates are strained to breaking point when Fish takes it upon himself to contaminate the jury pool by talking on camera to avid TV reporters. Not without cause does Bobby conclude that the lawyers at Cage/Fish are just crazed kids, and he privately urges Marie Hanson to drop them from the defence team.

Meanwhile, in a courthouse corridor, Renee has picked up a good-looking stranger, deliberately and ostentatiously dropping her briefcase in front of him. She asks if he would like to ask her out on a date and hands him her business card.

Later, dancing with him at the bar, she impetuously gives his backside a good squeeze and invites him home, where he proceeds to grope her aggressively. If Renee is surprised by this rather schematic turn of events, she's probably the only one: we've seen her recklessly lead him on and we realize she doesn't really know anything about him. When he ignores her plea to slow back down, she slaps him and he slaps her right back. So Renee, skilled kick-boxer that she is, knocks him unconscious. Still later, she's arrested for assault.

And still later, Renee is released on bail and Bobby apologizes for insulting the Cage/Fish team. And after that, Bobby comes to the bar, watching while Ally and the others have fun on the dance floor.

This is the first half of the two-part story that concluded on *The Practice*.

Original Airdate: 27 April 1998

Being There

Shocking, simply shocking, isn't it, when writers don't play fair, when an entire season's plot complications are revealed to be a dream sequence or a falsely accused character turns out to have an evil twin? It's not quite that bad here, but this is the episode that flunks the credibility test by resorting to the expedient of a faulty pregnancy test, even though, yes, it does happen in real life too.

When Ally, who with Cage will be representing Renee in court, notices that Georgia is carrying around a home pregnancy test, she pretends not to care, but we know better, and for those who might need reminding there's the special effect in which her face caves in.

In court, District Attorney Kevin Kepler (played by Eric McCormack, who went on to become Will in *Will & Grace*, NBC's sitcom about a gay man rooming with a heterosexual woman) questions Michael Rivers (Isaiah Washington), the man whom Renee kick-boxed into the hospital, who describes on the stand how Renee, 'oozing sex', invited him out on a date and then proceeded to leave him concussed, fractured and unconscious.

Cage's stomach-growling performance – using a clicker to make objections, wearing squeaking shoes – and apparently diffident cross-examination leaves Renee less than impressed, but Ally assures her there is a purpose for every Cage action, no matter how bizarre.

Back in court, Glenn, the well-endowed male model with whom Ally previously had sex, turns up to testify that Ally and Renee 'penguined' him by pulling down his pants and stranding him on the street under the pretence of a sexual advance.

Meanwhile, according to the home pregnancy kit, Georgia is pregnant, and she and Billy congratulate each other with incongruous politesse, shaking hands. Ally's reaction to the news is summarized quite neatly by the fantasy missile that blows through her, leaving a gaping special-effects hole.

Though Cage calls Renee to testify on her own behalf on the witness stand, he suddenly about-faces, telling the judge he won't examine her, and rests his case. Later, Cage explains that Renee is too hostile to make a good witness and that the prosecution put up a strong case, while the only way not to expose the defence's weaknesses is to not put up a case.

In his closing statement, though, Cage as ever shines, arguing that Renee had every right to tell Rivers no when he made a sexual advance, as well as to defend herself when Rivers, who is much bigger, slapped her.

Meanwhile, Cage has also suggested that Ally should choose a new, silly theme song to help her deal with the pain of Georgia and Billy having a child, and he recommends to her his own song, 'Lemon Tree'.

Ally chooses 'Wedding Bell Blues', which leads to a full-on musical number in the unisex bathroom, with showgirl-leggy secretaries singing and dancing their way into the stalls.

After Georgia tells Billy that the home test gave a false positive and she's not pregnant after all, he finds her weeping in the bathroom. Meanwhile, Renee admits to Ally that she's been using sex as a weapon ever since she was a girl.

Back at the courthouse, Renee, who'd been at risk of losing her licence to practise law if convicted, embraces Cage and Ally when the jury finds her not guilty.

Original Airdate: 4 May 1998

Alone Again

All the hopeful but unrequited lovers and starry-eyed dreamers at Cage/Fish and in the vicinity of the courthouse are alone again: not only the client who's suing for being left at the altar, and the client who tried to break out of prison on a home-made trampoline a mere month before his scheduled release, but Fish, who's longing for Whipper, and Cage, who's risking rejection by a former love of his life once again.

Cage agrees to represent Vincent Robbins, a 72-year-old career criminal, charged with attempted escape one month before his scheduled release after serving an eighteen-year sentence for bank robbery. Meanwhile, Fish and Georgia take on Mary Halliday, who wants to sue her ex-fiancé for emotional distress because he abandoned her at the altar, humiliating her before three hundred guests.

Cage and Ally meet Robbins in jail, and Cage seems to have come away from the meeting having picked up the old criminal's trait of blinking rapidly. Later, Cage bumps into the opposing counsel, DA Hayley Chisolm (played by Cynthia Stevenson), an old friend from law school who shares many of his quirks, and Ally promptly deduces that the pair may have been more than just friends. Later, Hayley tells John that their relationship was the best she ever had with a man, even if it was purely platonic, and Ally realizes that Cage was in love with Hayley, but never told her so.

Meanwhile, Georgia meets with Mary Halliday and advises her against going forward, but Fish interrupts and smoothly assures Mary that the ex-fiancé deserves to suffer for his actions. Georgia is incredulous: she knows the client has no case, but Fish blandly claims that once the proceedings turn ugly, Mary will beg them to settle, never knowing the firm was incapable of making good on its promises.

Later, Elaine approaches Mary with her latest invention – the Husband Compact Disc, on which is recorded all the customary sounds of a man around the house, from snoring to flatulence and a football game.

In court, a prison guard testifies that he witnessed Robbins trying to leap over the prison fence off his home-made trampoline, and that when Robbins fell and sprained his ankles, he was taken back into custody. On the witness stand later, Robbins explains that he collected and saved rubber bands for eighteen years so that he could assemble the trampoline. When he finally had it finished, he had to find out if it worked, he says, even though he was one month shy of being released. He claims he wasn't interested in escaping; he was just carrying out his dream.

In another courtroom, Whipper Cone presides over the Mary Halliday case, calling it one of the dumbest cases she has seen in her twenty years on the bench. Georgia suggests Cone should withdraw from the trial because of her past relationship with Fish, but Whipper insists she can remain impartial, and Fish argues that courts routinely enforce prenuptial agreements and arrange alimony payments. The ex-fiancé's lawyer agrees to make restitution for the wedding costs, but his client will not pay for emotional distress.

Before the negotiation gets any further, though, Whipper changes her mind and withdraws and, eventually, Mary decides to drop the suit, saying she doesn't feel sorry for herself any more, but feels sorry for Fish – because of his beliefs about marriage.

Meanwhile, Cage has told Ally that he asked Hayley out on a date a week before graduation from law school, but phrased it in such a way that she could have taken it – and did take it – as a joke. At the trial, Hayley offers to reduce the sentence facing Robbins to just four years, but he declines, believing he cannot accept guilt for the one thing in his life that makes him feel proud.

During closing arguments, Cage once again reminisces about his personal history, making the analogy between his feelings for Hayley and the courage it took for Robbins to try the leap over the prison fence. Though Hayley confirms Cage's fear that she never was in love with him, the jury sides with Robbins, and he is acquitted. In a final montage, we see all the would-be lovers and dreamers alone, even when they're in the office or when they're sitting together in the bar.

Original Airdate: 11 May 1998

These Are the Days

Bobby Donnell is back (from *The Practice*) looking for help with a case that involves two men – one rich and sick, the other poor and healthy – who want to force a hospital to perform an operation to switch their hearts, while Cage's cousin, a Cupid manqué, is arrested for assaulting happy couples by smacking them with a paddle. But most memorably, this is the episode in which Georgia decides to spice up her sex life with Billy by coming in nude to his room at the firm.

When Bobby turns up in the unisex to ask Ally if she would be interested in acting as co-counsel in the transplant case, Ally accepts, though she and her female friends can hardly maintain their composure around the handsome attorney from David E. Kelley's other lawyer show.

A plot about a poor man donating an organ to a rich one might've had any number of resonances with real social issues, but Kelley chooses to play this one conventionally, if not tritely, even. The poor man, Bernie Gilson, a former street person, wants to donate his healthy heart to ailing corporate executive Brian Michaelson not for money, or because he's being coerced in any way, but simply because over the years Michaelson has been kind to him.

In court, the judge reacts with disbelief when Bobby asks for a court order to force a hospital to perform the heart swap. The attorney representing the hospital argues that it could suffer damage to its reputation if the operation fails. Later, when Bobby and Ally are discussing the case, she convinces him to dance with her, a victory that Ally duly reports to Georgia in the unisex.

Georgia responds by saying she would have gone even further and kissed Donnell – a comment she regrets immediately, when Billy steps from a stall. It's just 'girl talk', she explains, but Billy thinks her remark shows a lack of regard for their marriage, and eventually they agree that their marriage is, indeed, in a rut.

Meanwhile, on the witness stand, Gilson describes how for years Michaelson would see him on the street and give him five dollars each week, and that one day Michaelson bought him some soup and they struck up a friendship, and that eventually Michaelson offered him a job. To repay him, Gilson tells the judge, he wants to give Michaelson his heart.

When it's Michaelson's turn on the witness stand, he says the only reason he's accepting the offer is for the sake of his family, and later Gilson tells Ally this is his chance to do something worthwhile for the first time in his life.

One night at the office door, Bobby and Ally exchange a meaningful look. Ally tells Bobby that she has a great imaginary world, 'but sometimes I just need things to happen for real'. And with that, Ally gives Bobby a kiss.

Eventually, the judge in the heart case makes a highly unusual decision: he appoints Ally judge, asking her to decide what is best for her client. Ally considers…and denies the plaintiff's motion, telling a disappointed Gilson that he need not sacrifice his heart to be someone.

Meanwhile, Cage's second cousin has been arrested for assaulting 'happy people' with a paddle. In court, couples testify that the cousin struck them when they were enjoying themselves in public, and when the cousin himself takes the witness stand, he daffily pronounces that he 'accelerates love' by striking lovers, and that he believes the incidents bring out the best in couples, whose relationships grow stronger as a result. Cage – for the first time since we've been watching *Ally McBeal* – loses the case.

Later, at the bar, Cage and Ally dance. Upstairs Georgia walks into Billy's office wearing nothing but shoes! They move into the conference room and begin making love.

Ally walks in on them, then turns off the lights and returns to her own office, where she remembers the events of the year and sheds tears of both joy and sadness.

Original Airdate: 18 May 1998

The Second Season

The Real World

In the real world a not-so-funny thing happened to *Ally McBeal* on the way to the second season: already on trial in the court of public opinion, standing accused of the murder of feminism, 'Ally' now faced the additional charge of being criminally thin, perhaps even wilfully starving herself. Regardless of how trying, rude, mean or intrusive all this seemed to the young actress at the centre of the media whirlwind, the show itself reaped even higher visibility and even higher ratings.

But now David E. Kelley, the master of multiple plots and ingenious twists on the controversial issues of the day, was forced to top improbable reality.

How well did he do right off the bat? Not badly at all in this first episode of the new season, in which Cage/Fish gets a new and even more stunningly beautiful young attorney and Ally finds herself attracted to an eighteen-year-old boy.

The road Ally goes down this time begins in a vivid dream. She is floating in darkness, her arm extended to a young man whose face is in shadow. As their fingertips touch, Ally awakes with a start.

Later that morning, she and Cage meet with Laura Jewell, a 39-year-old woman accused of having sex with Jason Tresham, now eighteen, who was only sixteen years old when their affair began, and Cage suggests that the best defence is an insanity plea.

When Ally encounters Jason in a court corridor, she hears chimes and is struck by...something, but is unsure just what her unsettled reaction means.

Meanwhile, Fish is explaining his own boyhood fixation on Shari Lewis, a perky blonde puppeteer on TV. Cage talks to him about an attorney named Nelle Porter (Portia de Rossi), a rising legal star nicknamed 'Sub-Zero Nelle' for her cool demeanour and ice-princess looks. She's looking to leave her firm, Cage says, and her client list is quite impressive.

In court, Ally questions Jason about how he met and fell in love with Laura Jewell, and she's taken aback by his sensitive responses and his emotional maturity. Some people find love, says Jason, while others are meant to be alone. To which Ally blurts out, 'What could be worse than being alone?' and ends her examination.

Later, Ally tells her therapist, Dr Tracy Clark, that she felt as if Jason was talking about her and admits she experienced impure thoughts about the young man. Dr Tracy takes her usual blunt tack, calling Ally a narcissist and pointing out that eighteen-year-old Jason is the same age Billy was, when Ally was dating him and believed he was the love of her life.

'To be thinking about an eighteen-year-old boy is not a cause for therapy,' says therapist Tracy.

Back in court, Laura Jewell takes the witness stand and describes in sensual, romantic detail her first sexual encounter with Jason. As Laura recalls how beautiful it was, Ally dissolves in a fantasy of making love to the boy and suddenly, caught up in fervency, lets out an embarrassingly audible squeak.

Laura tells the jury that she made love to Jason, at least in part, because he was a boy. 'Simple intimacy', she says, is what she got from the boy. When they first made love, 'he cried tears of joy'. Something within men dies emotionally as they grow older, she says, adding, 'Perhaps I was celebrating the boy inside him. I know I was celebrating the boy inside me.'

Still later, Ally expresses the wistful fear that she may be meant for a boy, not a man, and that's why she's fated to remain alone, and Billy tells her that perhaps she is meant to have a relationship with Jason.

Meanwhile, Nelle is hearing from Fish about the firm's guiding philosophy: 'Selfishism' is the firm's ideology, he says, and he tries to set an example there.

Later, confident Nelle, who has a forthright demeanour, approaches Georgia and Elaine, who quite obviously don't want her around. Nelle says she hopes to pick the brain of one of the firm's female employees before she decides whether or not to join.

Ally, Elaine suggests immediately, Ally McBeal will give you the 'straight dirt'. When Nelle leaves, both women agree that Nelle will hate Ally.

Later, Elaine tells Ally that Sub-Zero Nelle has a reputation for not holding out her hand very far when she meets someone, so that they will have to meet her more than half-way just to shake her hand.

And in a nice writerly touch that speaks volumes about both characters, when she and Nelle meet a moment later, neither one holds a hand out close enough for the other to grasp.

Ally tells Nelle that she enjoys working at the firm, but she believes she will never make partner, because the powers-that-be at Cage/Fish believe that women who want families will take maternity leave and eventually quit.

At the trial, Cage again reaches back to his own past for his closing argument, reminding the jurors of *Summer of '42*, a romantic Hollywood movie about the tender affair between a teenage boy and an older woman. 'It was beautiful,' he says of the point in the picture when the woman and the boy make love, 'and it was the ending we all wanted.'

After closing arguments, Ally hears from Laura that her relationship with Jason is over. Then Ally encounters Jason in the elevator and he tells her that she was in his dream the night before, that their fingertips were touching.

Naturally Ally rushes back to her therapist, who's dubious not only about the matching dreams but just generally about Ally, whom she quite obviously doesn't like.

'You can't hurry love' Vonda sings, and presently Ally hurries back to the courthouse to hear the Jewell case verdict: not guilty by reason of temporary insanity.

Afterwards, when Ally again encounters Jason in the elevator, she lets out another involuntary high-pitched squeak, and this time Jason asks her out on a date. To her own surprise (but to no one else's), Ally accepts, and when the elevator door opens, neither one moves to get out, both endearingly 'unsure' of their feet.

Meanwhile, Fish announces the inevitable to the staff: Sub-Zero Nelle Porter, who ironically was convinced by her little talk with Ally, has joined the firm. Afterwards, in a foreshadowing of what's to come, Cage admits to Alley that Nelle 'makes his heart go boom', even though he realizes she's the kind of woman he can only dream about, and later when he sees the ice princess letting down her tightly pulled helmet of white-blonde hair, her long tresses falling to her shoulders, he does indeed hear the beat.

That night, Jason and Ally go out. Jason tells Ally that his uncle is a groundskeeper at nearby Fenway Park, where the Boston Red Sox baseball team plays, and Ally, with excited girlishness, recalls how she and her father would listen to Red Sox games on the radio together when she was a kid and talks enthusiastically – perhaps more genuinely enthusiastic and unselfconscious than we ever saw her in the first season – about the crucial sixth game of the 1977 World Series.

In a rather charming scene over music, shot at night in the actual baseball park, vast and empty with its night-game lights blazing, the pair play a dreamy but energetic imaginary game of baseball – Ally in sweater, tennis shoes and jeans throwing, catching and batting the non-existent ball.

Afterwards, both flushed, Jason invites Ally up to his apartment, but Ally, ever the old-fashioned idealist, declines – it's a romance that could never be. They touch hands gently, the way they did in their matching dreams, and Ally gives Jason a final kiss goodbye. On the soundtrack Vonda sings 'In the Real World'.

Original Airdate: 14 September 1998

They Eat Horses, Don't They

If one ice princess heats up romantic complications at Cage/Fish, then what about two? Sub-Zero Nelle was supposed to bring new clients with her, and she has: this is the episode that introduces sub-zero chill personified, Ling Woo (Lucy Liu).

It's also the episode in which Ally goes on a Howard Stern-like 'shock jock' radio show.

Ling Woo, who we are informed manages a steel plant, is suing radio shock jock Harold Wick (Wayne Newton, in a brilliant piece of casting), who is clearly modelled after Howard Stern and his legion of imitators, right down to his crude and lascivious remarks to women. Ling (and don't forget to pronounce that name with the soft 'L'!) alleges that Wick's sexually charged programme spills over into her working environment, thereby contributing to sexual harassment at the steel plant.

After his racist- and sexist-epithet-filled deposition, Ally wonders aloud if the firm isn't giving Wick exactly what he wants: free publicity. Later, in court, his attorney argues that the lawsuit is preposterous because Wick's speech is protected by the First Amendment. But Nelle ripostes with an impressively ingenious argument, contending that Wick's words poison people's minds and create an atmosphere of gender bias in the same way that second-hand smoke poisons people's bodies.

Surprisingly, the judge doesn't throw the case out and an amazed and clearly jealous Ally later tells Elaine that Nelle's argument was brilliant.

Meanwhile, in court, we are learning about the episode's other case: John Cage is defending the owner of a French restaurant being sued by a man who took his wife there to celebrate their wedding anniversary and was distressed to discover that the chef's exotic menu included horse. Both the diner and his wife were nauseated, but on cross-examination, Cage points out that the plaintiff consumes cow, pig and even Cornish game hen without suffering the pangs of a guilty conscience. Says the diner: but the horse is a noble beast.

Later, we learn that it's a sentiment that Cage shares. He introduces Ally to Frawley, an old stuffed horse he's had since he was a boy – and isn't this a fine way of demonstrating that, in many ways, John Cage still is a rather-wizened boy? – then admits that he's always had a special feeling for horses.

Still later, the owner of the French restaurant takes the witness stand to insist that horse meat is low in fat and high in protein, and that he feels it is unjust for him to be dragged into court for serving it.

Meanwhile, courtesy of Fish, Nelle knows Cage is attracted to her. While Cage is working on his closing argument, Nelle shows up and he inquires if she has ever consumed horse meat. Nelle, rather sweetly, thinks she's being asked out on a date and, rather surprisingly to Cage, she agrees to meet for dinner.

And rather shockingly to Ally, the strategy Nelle and Ling cook up for the Wick case includes reading a statement to the media that implies Wick is impotent. Ally protests that what they did was dishonest, there's no evidence of any such thing, so later, when Wick invites Ally to appear on his programme, she accepts.

Meanwhile, at the horse meat trial, yet another heartfelt John Cage closing argument results in yet another victory – the jury finds in favour of the restaurant owner.

At the radio broadcast, Ally more than holds her own, and afterwards, she tells Wick that what the firm did to him in the press conference was underhand. Wick tells Ally that she's a good lady.

Original Airdate: 21 September 1998

Fools Night Out

How much of the off-beat charm and spark of a show like *Ally McBeal* is intended and how much is serendipitous and due only to lucky Hollywood stars? That Lucy Liu as Ling Woo is the former is abundantly demonstrated in this episode, only her second appearance. And that's surely a testament to the good judgement of David E. Kelley.

Liu as quirky, headstrong Woo is simply wonderful and her likes-attract fascination with selfishness-personified Fish, who pursues her because she's 'emotionally unavailable', is simply inspired. For that matter, so is the interwoven plot overall, which manages to combine bare female breasts with high-energy gospel music and a neat new twist in the Ally–Billy–Georgia triangle.

Unlike in theatrical films, where they are 'auteurs', directors in network series television tend to be hired hands, coming and going from episode to episode and show to show. But perhaps part of the credit this time should go to this episode's director: Peter MacNicol, who plays John Cage.

Back from the first season's episode about Fish's recently deceased uncle who hated short people are both the minister and choir soloist (the show-stopping singer Jennifer Holliday), only this time the minister is troubled after ending an affair with the soloist, who at services keeps breaking into pointed song about lost love and betrayal. The minister believes he cannot fire the soloist, because it might be perceived as retaliatory, and Fish promises he will drop by the church to observe.

Meanwhile, litigious Ling announces that she intends to sue a nurse who worked for a plastic surgeon. As it happens, Ling purchased breast implants as a Christmas gift for her sister, but only after the plastic surgeon showed off his nurse's perfect breasts, saying they were implants. But she and her sister were duped, says Ling, because in fact the nurse's breasts were natural. Scars make her sister vaso-vagal, says Ling tartly (by which she means looking at scars makes her sister faint). And suing the nurse isn't simply better television, we find, it's a better strategy: the surgeon is penniless and the nurse, says Ling, has an independent income.

Fish brings Ally and Renee to the minister's church, where the soloist belts out a powerful rendition of Al Green's 'Tired of Being Alone'.

Meanwhile, the nurse with the comely breasts admits that the plastic surgeon sometimes misrepresented her as someone on whom he had performed work. Her attorney then makes the rather spectacular suggestion to Billy and Georgia that they should compare their respective clients' breasts, side by side. Not surprisingly, Billy is enthusiastic, a fact that isn't lost on Georgia, who's already suffering from a bit of a 'mirror, mirror on the wall' complex because of the presence at the firm of the beautiful Nelle.

Ostensibly because she can 'tap into her despair', Ally has been tapped as mediator in the minister–soloist imbroglio, but talking to the soloist about her choice of music leads Ally to realize that her own situation with Billy is very much like Lisa's relationship with the minister. Each is working side by side with the man who broke her heart. Later, Ally realizes that, just like the minister with the soloist, Billy cruelly announced a change of heart with no advance warning. And then, walking down a Boston street, she suddenly stops in her tracks and, in a flashback to college days, realizes…Her break-up with Billy had nothing to do with him deciding to go to law school in Michigan! Billy, we are beginning to see, may not be entirely the paragon of Ally's memories.

Meanwhile in Billy's office, as the male lawyers ignore their own self-evident avidity (masquerading as professional detachment), both the nurse and Ling's sister take off their tops, while Georgia observes the performance with some dismay. Now, though, there's no doubt that the breast implant surgery turned out well and Georgia quashes the lawsuit, which, it turns out, Ling's sister wasn't too enthusiastic about in the first place.

Lawsuit or not, Richard knows he's interested in Ling and asks her out to dinner, while John, thinking about pursuing Nelle, professes to be 'buoyed' by Fish's advice to 'be yourself'.

That advice has resonance in a remark Fish makes to Ling, when he tells her they're alike. When he was a kid, people didn't like him either, Fish says, so he started being unscrupulous to feel in control of their reactions.

Meanwhile, Ally has deduced a betrayal in her past, and she tells Georgia so: Billy went to Michigan not for school, but to get away from her…and to be with someone who was already in Michigan at the time. Putting the pieces together, she concludes that Billy and Georgia met while Ally was still dating Billy. Georgia admits it's true and Ally is crushed.

Later, Georgia not only tells Billy that Ally knows about their Michigan affair, but that she now fears he may one day drop her just like he dropped Ally years earlier.

Meanwhile, Ally has convinced the church-choir soloist to sing at the bar and the minister to explain his feelings to her. Billy also tries to explain his long-ago feelings to Ally, telling her he knew he would marry Georgia ten minutes after they met, but insisting nothing happened between them until after he and Ally broke up. Ally accuses Billy of destroying her belief in hope, and shaking her conviction in the reality of the one love she thought she'd had in her life, and at the bar, the choir soloist takes the stage to sing an electrifying, and apposite, version of 'Fools Fall In Love'.

And so ends this affecting episode with the brittle, Stephen Sondheim-like musical sensibility.

Original Airdate: 28 September 1998

It's My Party

Is Ally a proper professional woman or a micro-miniskirt-wearing Super Freak?

Some time after his days as pratfalling Jack Tripper in the smirky sitcom *Three's Company*, John Ritter turned into a fine actor. His new-found soulfulness, skill and range were on display in such theatrical features as *Noises Off* and *Sling Blade*, and on the short-lived *Hooperman* TV series, and his talent is on display here, in his first outing as George Madison, the feminist-magazine editor fired for his Baptist (and therefore, presumably, fundamentalist) religious beliefs.

Ally's playfulness is on display too, in a scene in which she practises for the dinner party she and Renee are having by dancing around the flat to the sounds of 'Super Freak'. And David Kelley's ability to mix real-life controversy into a fictional plot is on display again, as well, when the judge in the Madison case holds Ally in contempt for disregarding his instruction not to wear short skirts in court.

Ally meets George by literally colliding with him, and she's immediately infatuated, but there's a complication, something she doesn't yet know, but begins to suspect later when – with George among those on hand – Elaine shows off her latest invention: customized condoms, each one with a different phrase that can be customized for its intended user.

Ally is offended that hers reads 'Take a Number', and suspicious when Elaine hands one to George that reads 'Been There', and gives him an affectionate kiss.

Later, in another outbreak of Cage/Fish surrealism, Ally shrieks when a bullfrog leaps up from a toilet seat and into her hair, at which point Cage bursts into the unisex to save Stefan, his pet, from harm. That Cage, a prince of a fellow who sometimes gets mistaken for a frog himself, should turn out to be an amateur herpetologist of all things, seems a particularly appropriate conceit.

George tells Ally that his boss, Catherine Hollings, believes that the Baptist faith runs contrary to the magazine's ideology, and in court her attorney maintains that it would be improper for an editor of a feminist magazine to hold the belief that a woman's place is in the home. The Baptist Convention, says the lawyer, declared that wives should submit to their husband's dominance in the home (which, in fact, it does in the world outside the show). Ally objects, saying that's only the case for Southern Baptists, and insists George believes men and women are equal.

Later, in chambers, the judge tells Ally every courtroom has a dress code and he insists she stop wearing miniskirts in his court.

But Ally defies him, continuing to wear her short skirts throughout the trial. Eventually, the judge rules for George, ordering the magazine to reinstate him. The judge then holds Ally in contempt of court, and instructs the bailiff to take her into custody.

When Ally refuses to apologize, she's forced to spend the night in jail. The next day, Ally appears again and calls the judge 'a pig'. Before she can be taken back into custody, Nelle presents an eloquent argument on her behalf, pointing out that despite Ally's 'inappropriate' attire, she still won George's case. The judge sets Ally free.

Most of the usual suspects, plus George, are at Ally and Renee's dinner party. The conversation takes an increasingly tense turn when Billy argues that women believe men cannot think clearly when they are aroused. The party seems about to dissolve into fiasco when the music begins and everyone starts dancing.

Fish and Ling finally have their first, passionate kiss. Meanwhile, the only obstacle to the attraction between Ally and George is the inconvenient fact that George is Elaine's boyfriend.

Original Airdate: 19 October 1998

Story of Love

You might think that an episode entitled 'Story of Love' would be about the Ally–Billy–Georgia triangle, but it's not. There is a triangle alright, but it's Ally–George–Elaine, and it results in another of the touching moments between Ally and her secretary, who otherwise is used mainly as comic relief.

The romantic complications among the main characters are echoed in this week's other case, which begins when Ally (yet again) tries to do the right thing for someone, but only ends up in jail. And oh yes, in this episode the story of the princess and the frog is back, so are the bagpipes, so is kick-boxing and so is the teary child-prodigy attorney.

On a Boston street, Ally encounters Hannah, a distraught young woman, sitting on the sidewalk. She offers assistance, but Hannah annoys her and the two get into an argument that escalates to blows, and Ally the kick-boxer drops her with a spin kick. Unfortunately, a policeman has seen it all and puts them both under arrest.

Of course, clients are where you can find them. When Ally and Hannah end up sharing the same cell, Hannah tells Ally how she's being sued for assault because she threw her best friend into a garbage bin after she discovered the best friend was having an affair with her boyfriend. When Ally and Hannah are released, Ally offers to represent Hannah in the assault case, but learns later that Hannah has fired three previous lawyers. Ally tries to back out, but it's too late.

Later, George Madison (John Ritter) decides to start his own magazine and wants Ally to do the paperwork. Elaine suggests Richard and Nelle instead, but George goes on to meet Ally and confesses his attraction to her.

Meanwhile, Cage has been training his pet frog for an upcoming competition. Cage dotes on his frog, but Nelle tells him she finds frogs repulsive. When the frog gets loose inside the unisex bathroom again, Billy, Fish and Georgia try to capture him, but Stefan hops into a toilet bowl. Inadvertently, Cage uses his remote flusher, but Billy, Fish and Georgia can't bear to tell him what's happened until later. When Fish finally tells him about Stefan's demise, Cage is devastated.

Later, Nelle, who is turning out to be a considerably less than icy princess after all, apologizes to Cage for her behaviour toward his frog. Like many another Cage/Fish denizen on many other occasions, she recalls an apposite childhood trauma. When she was a little girl, she explains, she had a hamster named Millie, whom she adored. But one day, her brother's Argentine horned frog ate her beloved hamster and she's hated frogs ever since.

Back in court, in the garbage-bin assault case, Oren Koolie, the weepy little-boy lawyer, pops up from under the plaintiff's table and, to Ally's surprise, recalls the time that Ally, momentarily deluded into believing he was a hallucination, kicked him.

Meanwhile, Cage has decided to hold a memorial service, complete with a dirge played on bagpipes, for Stefan the frog. At the service, however, Cage's sad farewell strikes his colleagues as hysterically funny. Later though, Nelle buys Cage a new pet frog, to which Cage takes an immediate liking, and in honour of her long-deceased hamster, he names it Millie.

Back in court, Ally can't fail to notice the parallels between Hannah's triangle and her own relationship with George and Elaine. In her closing argument, she berates little Oren Koolie and he begins to cry. Nonetheless, when the jury fines Hannah only one dollar for her assault, it's a victory for Ally.

In a touching moment, George tells Ally his feelings for her, and Elaine, who's overheard, begs Ally not to take away the man she loves. Later, George again approaches Ally in her office and Ally insists that she doesn't share his feelings, though quite clearly she does. And so George gets up and walks out of her life.

Original Airdate: 26 October 1998

Worlds Without Love

'Brief nudity. Viewer discretion is advised,' reads the message preceding this episode. The nudity, a full-length profile glimpse of Whipper Cone, is very brief indeed.

This is the episode about the straying nun and it ends with a boom-bada-boom one-liner, a hilarious joke about the very network that airs *Ally McBeal*.

That Cage/Fish has become a magnet for strange cases is obvious to everyone, even Ally, especially when she and Cage meet with Chrissa, an attractive, waif-like nun (in fact, she looks a bit like Ally herself) who 'made a mistake', and now wants to sue because she was 'fired' after she broke her vow of celibacy.

In the courthouse, Renee bumps into Matt, a handsome married man who, she later tells Ally, is her 'Billy'. In court, Chrissa describes how she met a man named Peter when she was doing charitable work at the homeless shelter he ran. One night, Chrissa relates to the silent, attentive spectators, while she and Peter were painting a room at the shelter, they found themselves staring at one another. 'Suddenly I had urges I was totally unprepared for,' she says. Then Peter kissed her and they made love. When the silence of the courtroom is broken by Ally blowing her nose, Judge Whipper Cone calls her into chambers and accuses Ally of resorting to a stunt. When Ally says she's coming down with a sinus infection, Whipper whips out a medical viewer and tells her to say 'Ah'. She also inquires, in an oh-by-the-way offhand manner, about Richard Fish and asks if he is dating anyone.

In a courthouse corridor, Renee sees Matt again and he tells her that his marriage has been a 'little bit bumpy lately'. Back in the courtroom, Chrissa is saying that if a priest had sex with a boy, he'd just be transferred, not dismissed as she was.

Meanwhile, back in the unisex bathroom at the firm, Georgia hears a noise coming from the toilet water below. She bends over for a better look, and suddenly, Stefan the frog leaps out and lands on her nose. Reflexively, Georgia hurls the frog away and it lands in Nelle's hair. Nelle swipes it off and she and Georgia bat it back and forth, until...

Cage's beloved frog lands splat against a stall. The lawyers sneak it out and a veterinarian puts the now-comatose frog on a respirator, but the Cage/Fish lawyers can't bring themselves to tell Cage what's happened.

Meanwhile, Renee and Matt have been reminiscing about old times. 'I fell out of touch because we couldn't keep in touch without touching,' she tells him in a typically clever bit of David Kelley word play, making it clear that she's not eager to resume the relationship.

Back in court, another nun is testifying that Chrissa's affair only ended when Peter 'dumped' her. This comes as a shock to Ally, who calls it not exactly a show of penitence.

Meanwhile, Ally takes it upon herself to dispense advice: to Whipper, whom she encourages to reconcile with Richard before it's too late; and to Renee, for whom, as a cautionary illustration of what will happen if she spends more time alone with Matt, she does an enthusiastic and credible orgasm imitation. Elsewhere, Fish has summoned enough courage to tell Cage about Stefan's dire condition.

After Ally goes to the church to talk settlement and is rejected, she goes into a confessional on a whim. Though she tells the priest she is only 'about a quarter Catholic', she then confesses to sleeping with any man with 'decent glutes' and to once going to bed with a man just because 'it' was big. 'I covet,' she says, admitting to her problem with the Tenth Commandment, and asks if 'on average' women having affairs with married men are happy.

That night, Fish has enticed Ling to his house. But when Ling opens the bedroom door, she sees...

In a room illuminated only by candlelight Whipper Cone, in full length profile, completely nude! Both women scream.

Later, in chambers, Ally visits the humiliated Judge Cone. To console her – and in a foreshadowing of a technique that her own therapist will use at a crucial juncture in a later episode – Ally tells Whipper to close her eyes and envision the perfect man, 'maybe on your wedding day', then imagine having to spend every day of the rest of your life with that same person. Whipper reacts predictably, going from 'aaah' to 'yech!'

Meanwhile, the church has decided to offer Chrissa her old job as nun back after all, because of the discovery that the priest to whom she had confessed the affair has been secretly videotaping parishioners' confessions using hidden cameras.

The priest, we are told with a straight face, aspires to become a television producer on the Fox Network (which in the world beyond the show actually airs *Ally McBeal*), and Fox has already offered him a 'slot' for his show to be called *The World's Naughtiest Confessions*.

Original Airdate: 2 November 1998

Happy Trails

Yes, savvy David Kelley surely noticed the dust-up that resulted when a critic charged that a first-season shot of Elaine's face at Ally's crotch level was a 'lesbian sight gag', so of course he contrived a slapstick complication that required them to kiss.

This is also the episode in which two of the many odd characters who come and go on this show are conveyed comically to the next world. One is Cage's dear frog, the other is cranky old Judge 'Happy' Boyle (in the world beyond the show, the actor who played him, Phil Leeds, actually did die).

When Cage barges into the unisex stall in which Fish is sitting to announce his resolve to give Nelle a first kiss, Nelle just happens to be eavesdropping.

Meanwhile, just the sight of Ross Fitzsimmons (comic Rob Schneider) entering the office with a bouquet of flowers horrifies Ally, who quickly explains to Elaine that she went out with the insufferable Ross the previous night. So Elaine forthrightly tells Ross that Ally has dropped dead. But Ross sees through her lie, so Elaine resorts to the ultimate emergency measure: she plants a kiss on Ally's lips, hoping to convince Ross that Ally is a lesbian.

Despite (perhaps because of) this bravura performance, Ally reluctantly agrees to go out with Ross on another date.

Elsewhere, Nelle has stopped by Cage's office to check on Stefan the frog, who seems to be coming along nicely. But Cage, overwrought in his own way, accuses her of having assaulted Stefan with a file folder. Demonstrating said assault, he picks up a file and swats the hapless Stefan out of the window. Luckily, the frog lands on a ledge and Ling comes to the rescue with a small box dangling from a piece of string. The dazed frog hops inside.

Meanwhile, Billy and Georgia have met with Joanne Poole (played by Melanie Chartoff), an orange-coloured woman (don't ask: too many carrots, perhaps, or a genetic disposition; the important thing is that she's found her way to the right firm) who has lost her job because of – what else? – the colour of her skin.

In court, Billy and the opposing lawyer argue over whether or not orange skin is within the scope of the civil rights law. Later, Judge 'Happy' Boyle is about to rule when...He pitches forward and dies.

Meanwhile, most of the Cage/Fish lawyers haven't yet heard about the judge's death: Nelle has invited Cage, Ling and Fish out to dinner to celebrate Stefan's rescue, and Cage of course brings the recuperating frog along. Elaine has urged Ally to be more forceful with Ross, to give him unalloyed the 'straight hard dump'.

At a Chinese restaurant where they're dining, Cage asks Ling to ask the Chinese-speaking waiter to feed Stefan some lettuce and then bring him back to the table. Uh-oh. Later, when Cage asks Ling to ask the waiter for Stefan, the all-too-obvious punch-line ensues: Stefan was the main course!

Outraged, Cage addresses his fellow restaurant patrons, giving a brief synopsis of the many tragedies that befell the brave-but-misbegotten amphibian. At the end of his heartfelt oration, the patrons are confused at first, then they applaud politely.

Meanwhile, Ally's date with Ross turns out to be even worse than she had imagined, and when she and Renee (who's been coerced into chaperoning) get word of the Happy Boyle tragedy, it's just the excuse they need to flee.

Later, when persistent Ross returns to the firm, Elaine convinces him to hop around on one foot while blowing on a whistle. Then she poses the compelling question: Why would an attractive woman like Ally settle for a dumpy-looking man who hops around blowing a whistle? Humiliated, Ross departs, only to return later to meet the fetchingly orange Joanne.

Trying to comfort Cage about the death of his frog, Nelle assures him that she didn't find Stefan at all tasty. She describes it as tasting 'a little tough'. Cage's reaction is laughter, followed by sadness, which makes Ally realize that it's perhaps the eccentrics – people like John Cage and Happy Boyle, who had a fixation with teeth – who are to be most treasured in this world.

At Judge Happy's funeral, Jennifer Holliday and the gospel choir again sing. At the podium, Billy tells the mourners that it would make Happy happy if they showed him their teeth, and so they do, in a tribute to the odd old judge.

When Cage walks Nelle to the door of her house, he's nervous and she's tired of waiting. She gives him a kiss, sending him dancing into the night.

Original Airdate: 9 November 1998

Just Looking

This is the episode that adds mud wrestling-club owner to the resumé of the redoubtable Ling (and don't ever forget that soft 'L') and also introduces the helpful phrase 'dumb stick' to the viewing public. So is it any wonder that Cage and Fish volunteer to go 'just looking'?

A civic group called MOPE – Mothers Opposed to Pornographic Entertainment – is seeking to close Ling's mud wrestling establishment down. But Cage and Fish fearlessly volunteer to go undercover on a fact-finding mission for the firm to make certain, as Nelle cautions them to do, that there's no nudity or sexual touching allowed.

Meanwhile, Elaine demonstrates her newest invention, the high-tech toilet, which features a seat warmer, an auto-flusher and a seat that can be raised and lowered with the push of a button on a remote-control device. It is, of course, the perfect toy for John Cage.

As it turns out, MOPE's attorney is Raymond Brown, Georgia's old boyfriend, who is an eligible bachelor and still quite interested in her. And as it happens, both Georgia and Ally find Raymond's demeanour and looks quite intriguing too. In fact, when Georgia introduces him, Ally is so tongue-tied she can't even stammer out her own name properly, saying 'beat, meat' and so forth.

Georgia arranges a date for Ally and Raymond, and before going out on it Ally stops at home for her 'lucky' underwear. Meanwhile, in court, one of the MOPE members calls mud wrestling degrading to women and Nelle counters that adult movies often feature steamy sex scenes.

Back at the firm, in the unisex, Ally sits down just as Cage uses the remote to make the seat rise, and Ally plunges into the bowl. It's a broad enough visual joke made droll by the added real-world association in the viewer's mind: Ally cannot extricate herself from the toilet because she's too thin.

Meanwhile, as 'Secret Agent Man' plays, Cage (in a trench coat) and Fish make their way into Ling's mud wrestling club, where Fish outbids the other men in the audience for a chance to wrestle one of the beautiful females, who, under their coats of slick mud, are wearing one-piece bathing suits. In the match Fish's opponent rubs his face between her mud-covered breasts.

Ally, finally extricated, and Raymond make their way with Billy and Georgia to the bar. When Raymond and Georgia dance, Ally begins to suspect that they might still be attracted to one another. Afterwards, Georgia admits to Ally that she misses the little 'date highs' in the days before her marriage and Ally warns her that what she is doing with Raymond is, in its own way, an affair.

Back on the witness stand, Ling defends her club, insisting that her wrestlers make good money by teasing men, who are at the mercy of their 'dumb stick'. Her wrestlers make nearly $100,000 a year, she says proudly. 'The drunken Neanderthals throw money at them,' she says, adding rather magisterially that women are already exploited by everything from high-heel shoes to painted eyelashes.

Says Ally: Ling is her hero, but Nelle is not so impressed and turns the closing argument over to Richard, so he can give the 'dumb stick point of view'.

In the meantime, Nelle calls a male stripper to the witness stand. He's an attorney, he says, but he prefers the life of a dancer because of the money, and because of the gratification he receives from women responding to his looks. Nelle asks him if he'd feel like a victim if she said all she wanted to do was lick every inch of his body with her tongue until she was dehydrated. Quite sensibly the stripper replies that he'd 'get over it'.

In his closing speech, Fish argues that being in a room filled with other men ogling women is a liberating experience, because sexual desire is not deviant, it's normal. 'Once a man hits puberty,' Fish argues in one of the clever, contrary arguments that David Kelley writes for him, 'he gets a sense that he'll always be part idiot.' Sex clubs, therefore, preserve male mental health. The judge agrees, saying that maybe popular entertainment really does reflect community standards, and Ling wins the case.

Afterwards, Raymond and Georgia end up in the same elevator, and Raymond hits the stop button and asks Georgia for just one kiss, so he will once and for all know what it would have been like if they had pursued their relationship. Georgia declines and Raymond turns the power on, and a moment later Georgia turns it back off. As 'One Fine Day' plays on the soundtrack, they have a quick, chaste 'going nowhere' almost-kiss.

Original Airdate: 16 November 1998

You Never Can Tell

You never can tell what someone's thinking – or can you? If you thought Ally stuck in the toilet bowl was amusing, then wait until you see her with her hand caught in a bowling ball. And if you liked the pretending-to-be-a-lesbian ploy to get rid of an unwanted suitor before, wait until you see it this time. And oh yes, there's another improbable lawsuit involving Ling and more about the frog too.

Doing a weekly one-hour series is brutally paced work, so it's not surprising that sometimes a writer as busy as David Kelley will repeat a good gag. What's surprising is how well the *déjà vu* works.

As Thanksgiving approaches, Ally 'hears' the song 'I Know Something About Love', and indulges in her own private tradition: giving 'thanks' for all the things she doesn't have, such as a lover, by kicking and tossing cushions and pillows around.

At Cage/Fish it's another typical day: Elaine is modelling her latest invention, a pregnancy dress, which will allow all women to share the societal benefits of pregnancy, such as avoiding speeding tickets; and Ling, who pronounces herself 'penile psychic' (meaning she can tell what a man's thinking with his 'unit'), wants to sue an employee for having sexual thoughts about her. Furthermore, she tells lust-smitten Richard she now wants him to call her by food endearments.

Meanwhile, Nelle, especially fetching with her hair down and wearing a Ling-designed outfit called The Steward, asks tongue-tied Cage out on a date (he has to nose-whistle his yes), and Renee fixes Ally up with a blind date at a bowling alley.

In court, Ally counters the opposing attorney's argument that it's ridiculous to sue his client simply for having sexually harassing thoughts by giving appraising looks to his backside and flirting seductively with the judge who, getting her obvious, unspoken point, allows the case to proceed.

Ling testifies that she was unable to fire the employee because of the union and she claims she is pursuing legal action against him to prevent harm to future victims.

Meanwhile, Cage's date with Nelle fizzles out when another man tries to pick her up and John gives up. It's nothing, though, compared to the fiasco that awaits at the bowling alley: not only is Wally, her date, a nerd of epically annoying proportions, but when Ally can't find a ball that will fit her tiny fingers, a wizened old man offers her his most treasured possession, his dead wife's bowling ball. Of course, her fingers get stuck, and of course persistent Wally gets stuck on her.

Cut to the emergency room, where a doctor suggests that the bowling ball be cut, but the little old man begs Ally not to destroy his treasure, which is why the next morning in court...

The judge instructs the jury that the bowling ball has no legal relevance to Ling's case. In their closing arguments Ally and Georgia insist the case is not about the man's salacious thoughts, it's about how he communicated those thoughts. In a directed verdict, however, Ling loses.

Back in the office, Cage offers Nelle a heartfelt metaphor: 'I let my frog roam free,' he says. 'It got flushed down the toilet.' Now he fears that Nelle will do the same thing to his hope.

With floundering love lives in the balance, efficient Elaine takes charge, offering courting advice to Cage: all women really want is to be pulled onto the dance floor.

Then when Wally, 'the most boring man on Earth', appears Georgia goes into Ally's office and, a beat later, Elaine escorts Wallace inside. When the door opens, Ally and Georgia are 'caught' kissing; horrified, Wallace says he will 'pray for' Ally and he runs off. 'Ding-dong, the bore is gone,' says Elaine brightly, while Ally, taking mock umbrage, accuses Georgia of giving her tongue. Georgia denies it, but Ally insists: 'A flutter,' she says.

Later, at the bar, Ally tells Renee that staging the kiss was the only way to get rid of the homophobic Wallace, but that Georgia is a pretty good kisser.

As Vonda begins to sing 'It was a teenage wedding' from the Chuck Berry song 'Never can Tell', Ally, Renee and Elaine dance together – 'A little three-way?' asks Ally blithely. 'I'm in,' says Elaine – while Cage, just as instructed, pulls Nelle onto the dance floor.

Original Airdate: 23 November 1998

Making Spirits Bright

Heard the one about the virgin and the unicorn? Well, Ally may not be a virgin exactly, not as scientists measure these things, but she does remain pure in spirit. Otherwise, how would she be able to tame the mythical wild horse?

This is the Christmas episode about Cage, Nelle and the mistletoe, and about Ally and the unicorn. It's also the episode with the Lara Flynn Boyle cameo. Boyle, who plays Helen Gamble in *The Practice*, David E. Kelley's other Boston lawyer show, is as thin as Calista and has been the subject of anorexia rumours too. When Helen and Ally meet in the elevator, they exchange hostile looks and knowing badinage about eating a cookie. Peter MacNicol directs skilfully again.

When Cage notices Nelle standing beneath mistletoe, he stalks her, intending to steal a kiss, but at the last moment she senses his presence and turns to him, which is when Billy interrupts to announce that Sheldon Maxwell (played by Mark Linn-Baker), Fish's biggest client, has been fired from his job as a bond trader. Later, Maxwell explains that he lost his job after telling his colleagues that he saw a unicorn in his office

Ally, for a reason we will learn later, is moved by this news.

Elsewhere, Matt, Renee's 'Billy', is back, pursuing her again with characteristic ardour. Later, Ally walks into Renee's bedroom, interrupting Renee and Matt making love. Back at Cage/Fish, Ling shows up, distributing Christmas gifts and radiating uncharacteristic good cheer. But no one seems properly responsive, and Elaine explains to Ling that nobody believes she is capable of goodwill. In the episode after next, however, we will see just how deeply Ling can be touched emotionally.

With Judge Whipper Cone presiding, the unicorn case gets under way. In court, Billy argues that Sheldon's unicorn sighting hasn't affected his job performance, but the brokerage house's attorney counters that investors could file a lawsuit if they thought a delusional employee had cost them their fortunes. When Sheldon himself takes the witness stand, he describes his first encounter with the unicorn in his office and says that none of his colleagues could see the mythological creature.

Later, Billy remembers that when he and Ally were seven-year-olds, she said she'd seen a unicorn. When Sheldon's boss testifies, Billy wonders what would have happened if Sheldon had seen a vision of Jesus Christ instead of the mythological horse, which is also regarded as a symbol of Christ. Simply seeing an apparition, Billy argues, is not grounds for dismissal.

Later, Sheldon and Ally meet, and he senses that she's seen a unicorn, too. People who have seen the creature are lonely and have virtuous hearts, he says, and Ally recalls how she petted the animal, as only the pure of spirit can do.

In his closing argument, Billy calls the unicorn a holiday symbol of hope. Whipper agrees and Sheldon wins back his job.

Meanwhile, Matt tells Renee he's leaving his wife, who is pregnant, and so Renee leaves him. Later, Ally, agreeing that Renee could get hurt, tells her that 'common sense is killing us', and wonders if perhaps she should have stayed with Matt.

While the Cage/Fish attorneys gather for a holiday party, another occasion for musical numbers, Renee tells Matt she is determined not to allow him to destroy her, and then she sends him out alone.

Back at the party, Cage is trying the mistletoe manoeuvre again. This time, when she sees him, Nelle gives him a passionate kiss. Later, as Ally walks through the empty office to the elevator, she sees a unicorn. Petting the mythological creature, she wishes it a Merry Christmas.

Original Airdate: 14 December 1998

In Dreams

Of all the odd and oddly touching cases that wash up at Cage/Fish, this may be the most melancholy and touching of all, particularly for dreamy, lovelorn Ally. It's the story of a dying woman who prefers her dreams to her waking life, and who seeks to force a hospital to place her in a medically induced coma so she can spend the last months of her life with her fantasy lover. Her doctor, of course, turns out to be none other than Greg Butters (Jesse L. Martin), Ally's would-be new dream man.

The ill woman is Ally's old high school teacher, Bria Tolson, a frail but mentally alert seventy-year-old whom Ally visits in the hospital. Her priest is there too, and as Ally and he talk, Bria drifts off and begins hallucinating, conversing with Henry, the imaginary man who lives only in her dreams.

A bit later, Bria tells Ally that she and Henry married and had a family in her dreams. When Bria's eyes close, the machines monitoring her vital functions sound sudden warning beeps and a doctor charges into the room to revive her. But a moment before he applies the defibrillator, Bria comes to, even though the monitor continues to show a flatline. The doctor realizes that a monitoring wire merely became disconnected, and Ally realizes that the doctor is none other than Greg Butters. And for viewers who need confirmation of how Ally feels about suddenly seeing the man she suspects could supplant Billy in her heart, there's a quick lizard-tongue fantasy moment.

Greg tells Ally that Bria has only a short time left to live, and Bria tells Greg that she would like to go to sleep – and never wake up – so that she can spend her remaining time in her dream world with Henry and her children. When Ally pursues the idea of a medically induced coma, Greg assures her the hospital would never approve, but Ally forges ahead, going before Judge Whipper Cone to argue that when Bria goes to sleep, she enters a better place.

Meanwhile, back at the firm, Nelle, not easily deterred, has approached hapless John Cage in the unisex, seductively telling him how public places excite her. When she undoes his necktie, Cage flees. Later, Ling offers Fish her opinion that Cage is gay, but Fish points out that no one thinks a woman is homosexual just because she rebuffs a man's advances.

Meanwhile, Whipper has agreed to speak with Bria in her hospital room, where Bria recounts how she first invented Henry when she didn't have a date for the high school prom, but as time went on just couldn't wait to fall asleep to be with her imaginary lover in his better world.

Whipper rules that Bria is of sound mind, but the hospital still refuses her request for an induced coma, so Ally goes after a court order.

At the hearing, the hospital's chief of staff claims that it's ethically wrong for the hospital to intentionally place a patient in a coma and that there's no guarantee the comatose person would continue experiencing dreams. But Ally counters that hospitals increase morphine drips to accelerate the deaths of terminally ill patients and wonders why, therefore, it's an ethical problem to help a patient fall asleep.

Back at the firm, Nelle consults her 'inner world' too, and has a vision of Cage thrown into a dumpster bin, so she tells him their relationship is over. Later Ling, in her own frosty way, says that Nelle likes Cage because she knows he will never find her 'defrost button'.

Meanwhile, Bria has temporarily left the hospital to attend final arguments in the courtroom, where the hospital's attorney is arguing that allowing her to be put into a coma would set a bad precedent. Ally counters that the court shouldn't consider the bigger picture, but rather it should rule on Bria's particular circumstances. After Bria tells Whipper that not waking up again doesn't frighten her, Whipper grants her request for a trial period of one week.

Back at the office, Cage, summoning a timid bravery, tells Nelle he's willing to risk their present relationship by progressing beyond the platonic stage.

At the hospital, while Ally watches, Dr Greg puts Bria into the induced coma. And as Bria drifts off, Ally notices a little smile is playing on her face.

Original Airdate: 11 January 1999

Love Unlimited

Unlimited love? Not in this episode about a case involving a sleazy husband who wants to annul his marriage on the ground that 'sexaholism' made him incompetent to agree to marriage, and certainly not when Dr Greg returns from Chicago either.

'Anticipation' is playing on the soundtrack when Greg walks Ally to her front door. It's a new beginning, he says, to which Ally replies, 'I like that word, "begin",' and their two special-effects lizard tongues flick slowly towards one another.

The next morning, Ally is so happy at this turn of events that she feels ten feet tall – which we know for certain when we see her coming out of the elevator at the firm: she is in fact approximately ten feet tall, and has to duck her head to get through the lift door. But it lasts only until she sees Ling, who quickly brings her down to size, announcing irately that she intends to sue the environment.

As it happens, an environmental group is suing Ling over a housing project that she is developing. Since the activists claim that trees have rights, Ling has decided to counter-sue the environment.

Meanwhile, Fish and Ally take the case of Kimberly Goodman, whose husband wishes to annul their nine-year marriage on the grounds of sexaholism-induced incompetence.

When Ally suddenly decides she needs emergency therapy, saying, 'I think I need mental help. I feel happy and I'm not equipped,' Cage invites her to share his appointment with Dr Tracy, who turns out to be unavailable.

Instead, they meet with bow-tied, bespectacled Dr Nickle (played by Bruce Willis). But he turns out to be even ruder and more blunt than Dr Tracy, and when he calls Cage 'Stuttering John' (a reference to one of Howard Stern's cronies), Cage and Ally leave, affronted.

Meanwhile, Fish complains to Ling that after dating for four months they have yet to have sex. 'Whatever happened to emotional intimacy?' Ling replies, saying she likes foreplay. And to prove it, she licks Fish's finger erotically.

'See,' says Ling, 'there are so many things beside intercourse, but men just can't see beyond their dumb sticks.' She leaves the thoroughly boggled Fish holding his finger stiffly in front of his face.

Later, Ling tells Nelle she never even says the word 'sex', because it drives men – and even some women – crazy. Nelle convinces her to say the word…and realizes that she is telling the truth.

Elsewhere, in the first of a pair of witty jokes about the furore and controversy in the wider world beyond the show, Ally runs into a pushy woman who announces she's an editor at *Pleasure* magazine, where they've elected Ally as a working-woman role model. But, she blathers on, 'we do not want you to be skinny'.

Ally's eloquent reply: she bites off the woman's nose!

Immediately after, Ally and Cage decide to have their own therapy session sans therapist, and Ally describes her 'dream' (which we've just seen) in which a female executive announces that Ally has been elected a role model and Ally responds by biting off the executive's nose. Then, in a wry reference to the did-Ally-kill-feminism cover story in *Time* magazine, Ally tells Cage she even dreamt that they put her face on the cover of *Time* magazine as the 'face of feminism'.

Ally concludes by changing her theme song from 'Tell Him' to 'Ooh-Ooh Baby'.

Meanwhile in court, where Kimberly's husband is on the stand and Fish is pointing out that his sexaholism claim is an obvious ploy to escape making alimony payments, while a psychiatrist, testifying for the husband, claims that sex addicts suffer from a compulsive disorder and, because of childhood abuse, he experiences bouts of powerlessness that extended to his decision to marry.

When Kimberly takes the witness stand, she testifies that only after she finally realized that her husband was hopelessly addicted to sex, and she filed for divorce, did Stanley attempt to annul the marriage.

Back at the unisex, in another witty moment, Fish and Cage are practising their Barry White dance moves in front of the mirror. First Elaine, then Ling join in and they're all dancing in a line, until Nelle appears and they go crashing down to the sound effect of struck bowling pins.

That night, Cage sets out on his new spontaneity plan to win Nelle, entering her office when they're alone and giving her a meaningful gaze. Nelle, who's overheard his intentions, responds by wordlessly stepping out of her dress. But when she unhooks her bra, Cage stutters, 'I, I can't,' and flees the room.

'It wasn't performance anxiety,' Cage, a popsicle in his hand, insists later to Ally.

Back in court, Ally gives an impassioned closing statement, shaming the husband for subjecting his wife and children to public embarrassment. 'Little Mister Helmet Head,' she scoffs. 'This man...parading his penis' like a handicap sticker. 'You giant ass!' she declares and the audience in the courtroom erupts in applause.

The judge denies the annulment petition.

Later, when Cage tries to apologize to Nelle, she replies, 'You've met somebody' – a reference to Ally – and leaves the room. To John it's a revelation.

In a musical interlude, Vonda sings 'Apple, peaches, pumpkin pie...Ready or not, here I come.' Then, while Ally and Greg walk through the snowy Boston streets, she tells him that her favourite song in high school was the sentimental 'Can I Have This Dance?' and Greg tells her that he believes in the concept of marriage, intending to marry only once. This brings a slight smile to Ally's face, and as 'Can I Have This Dance?' plays, we see in triple split-screen:

Cage musing at a window...

Ally and Greg walking in the romantic snow...

Nelle alone, striding down the street.

Original Airdate: 18 January 1999

Angels and Blimps

Of all the *Ally* episodes, surely this one, about the brave dying child who wants to sue God, is the saddest.

For comic relief, though, there's Cage and Fish, bumping heads together, trying a murder case.

When Greg and Ally stroll down a hospital corridor together, she feels as if she's walking on air (we know because we see here up there), but it only last until she unexpectedly encounters Ling, which immediately brings her to earth.

Ling momentarily morphs into the slavering creature from *Alien*, then snaps at a man in a wheelchair: 'It's bad enough you people get all the parking spots!'

As it happens, Ling is in the hospital to retrieve the flowers she sent to a sick friend who died, she says.

When Dr Greg stops in to check on eight-year-old Eric, who has leukaemia, the boy at first thinks Ally is an angel.

Later, at the firm, Nelle turns up wearing the Rocky Raccoon look – brown make-up all around her eyes, so that she seems to be wearing goggle-like glasses. 'Just felt like it,' she shrugs, and the quirky bit of business is taken no further.

When Fish and Cage elect to try an attempted-murder case themselves, not only Billy is sceptical. The prosecutor, Renee, who asks why Billy isn't part of the defence, is as well.

'The question smacks of commentary, Renee,' Cage sniffs, giving the droll line a nicely understated delivery.

Later, Ally meet Eric's mother Julie, who explains that Eric's father was killed by lightning and that their insurance company won't pay for the experimental treatment that might save Eric. Later, Eric himself asks Ally to sue God.

Ally demurs, but Ling interrupts to assure the little boy that, of course, he can sue the Almighty. After all, wasn't Eric's father killed by an act of God and isn't Eric's church the house of God? Therefore, Ling concludes, sue the church.

Later, Nelle informs her stunned colleagues that Ling is a non-practising attorney, and that she was editor of the *Law Review* at Cornell.

Meanwhile, at the murder trial, Rodney is on the witness stand, explaining how he was in bed with his friend Harvey's wife when Harvey – Cage and Fish's client – caught them together and began shooting. Rodney was wounded, but recovered from his injuries.

At the firm, Ally reluctantly agrees to represent Eric against the 'defendant' – and she points heavenwards – while Eric says bitterly, 'There is no God...like Santa Claus.'

Ally reveals that she had a baby sister who died at the age of five, and that after she stopped believing in God, until the first time she saw a blimp and her mother told her that blimps were made to remind people that God is up there. Now, every time Ally sees a blimp, she thinks of the Almighty.

Ally also wants Ling on the defence team, but Ling at first refuses, saying, 'Practice causes wrinkles – look at you.' But later, of course, she relents.

In court, Renee questions Dr Burns, who testifies that Harvey's anger never rose to the level of insanity. Fish, in his own unique way, cross-examines the doctor. He gets Burns to admit that he has been wrong in the past.

When Ally and Ling meet with the lawyer for Eric's church, he scoffs at the idea of suing 'God's house', but Ling makes a compelling case that because Eric's parents had contributed generously to the church, there was a duty for the church to give back to the boy, and that the cost of defending the church's position would cost more than simply settling and paying for his experimental treatment.

To Ally's surprise, the church settles, and with money no longer an issue the experimental treatment that may save Eric's life can begin.

Later, with Dr Greg, Ally recalls her New Year's resolution – 'Less fantasy, more reality' – as she slides onto his lap and kisses him.

Meanwhile, at the attempted-murder trial, Cage in his closing argument remember April 4, 1977, the day in high school he finally summoned the courage to ask the most beautiful girl in his class to the prom and, to his surprise, she said yes. That was the day he realized the mind could produce mind-altering chemicals. Two days before the prom, the girl changed her mind, Cage continues, posing the question of what it must have been like for Harvey to have committed his life to someone and then to find that person in bed with another man. 'A gentle, law-abiding man committed an insane act,' he says to the jury, pleading that Harvey be found not guilty by reason of temporary insanity.

Renee scoffs, calling Cage and Fish 'Mutt and Jeff lawyers' and their defence 'achy-breaky heart', but the jury agrees with Cage, and Harvey is found not guilty.

The most surprised people in the courtroom are Cage and Fish, who bump heads trying to pick up their briefcases at the same time.

Meanwhile, Eric has taken a turn for the worse and is dying. Both Ally and Ling visit him a final time in the hospital. When Dr Greg tells them that – off camera – Eric has passed away, Ally responds bitterly.

'There is no God,' she says.

'This isn't the world's biggest shock,' Ling snaps at her. 'Get over it.'

Then, over Vonda rainbow music, Ling runs from the room and breaks into tears.

While the music continues, we see a special-effects shot of a glowing, pyjama-clad boy being led by a giant hand from above. As the boy guided by the hand walks away from us, he disappears through a wall.

Later, Billy offers to walk the distraught Ally home. 'I'm going to go solo,' she replies, setting off down the streets. Looking up outside, she spots a blimp – 'Just Looking' flashes in neon on its side – but, lost in momentary wonder, she doesn't notice that Ling, whom we are to presume ordered up the blimp, is watching from nearby.

Original Airdate: February 8, 1999

Pyramids on the Nile

There's no question that Cage/Fish & Associates has become a firm known for specializing in sexual harassment law. When a large and prestigious company fires two employees for breaking its 'date and tell' office policy, it's Nelle and Cage versus the company's squad of seven matching attorneys.

Meanwhile, Dr Greg has shown up at the firm with Valentine's Day flowers. Ally is immediately struck by a quiverful of arrows fired by a Cupid who looks suspiciously like the Dancing Baby, while Billy is immediately struck by jealousy when he sees Ally and Greg kiss.

Ling decides she wants to come out of retirement and become an associate at the firm. Fish's reluctance lasts only until she convinces him by seductively sucking his finger. When Fish announces his decision to make Ling 'of counsel', he does it with exemplary Fishian brevity: 'Asset, firm, bygones,' he says.

Later, while they're playing Go together, Fish tells Ling he'd 'do almost anything to introduce my penis to the inner you'. And still later, to the accompaniment of 'Mustang Sally' on the soundtrack, Ling gives Fish 'hair' and hot wax – a bit of hot candle wax and a whiskery tickle down his bare chest with her long mane.

Meanwhile, Ally and Billy are thrown together on the case of Myra Jacobs (played by Anna Nicole Smith, an actress/model who in real life became famous for marrying a rich, and elderly, man), who is contesting a will that would cut her out of a fortune if she remarries.

Later, after a ruling goes against her, Billy lashes out at Ally, calling her 'unprofessional to the point of malpractice' for going out on a Valentine's Day dinner with Greg rather than preparing for the case.

In court, Nelle and Cage's client, Steve, testifies as to how he met and fell in love with Callie Horn at the company where they both worked. When the company's personnel vice-president asked them about their affair, they admitted the relationship and were summarily discharged for not adhering to the strict policy called 'date and tell', under which employees are required to disclose their love affairs with other employees, thereby protecting the company against sexual harassment claims. Another lawyer specializing in sexual harassment cases calls the company's policy excellent and identical to the one many other large companies use.

Later, Billy confesses that he still loves Ally, telling her, 'Whatever we become, we can't be anything but truthful with each other...I can't keep it to myself any more.'

To which she replies: 'I think you should have.'

While Vonda sings of a 'hundred tears' on the soundtrack, Ally runs home. There, she tells Renee that her time before Dr Greg and without Billy was 'quality time loneliness', and adds that 'even if I knew my feelings, the last thing I would do is trust them'.

At the firm, when Georgia comes to talk to her on some minor matter, Ally pratfalls all over the place with nerves. In the unisex, Ally and Billy (literally) bump into each other, and Ally says that she's falling in love with Greg, but still feels that she and Billy were 'meant for each other'.

Back in court, Cage has had an inspiration and puts Ling on the witness stand to testify about her own sexual harassment suit.

In his closing argument Cage tells the jury about his own efforts to date Nelle, his co-counsel, and argues that Steve and Callie were fired for simply trying to keep their private life private. 'Have we all gone mad?' he asks with some feeling. 'Do you know how hard it is to find love,' and you take away the workplace? It's an argument the jury sympathizes with, and the company is ordered to pay $942,000.

Naturally, Cage/Fish triumphs in its other case as well, and Fish is moved to tell the press that 'justice is never more sweet than when you get it on one-third contingency'.

To keep from thinking about Billy, in the office Ally listens to Boz Scaggs singing 'Georgia' on headphones. Later, she arranges a dinner date with Greg. When she sees Billy (who looks red-eyed, as if he'd been crying) standing in the doorway, Ally says, 'I really like him.'

'I just didn't think you could find the person of your dreams at age eight,' says Billy. And, while 'You Belong to Me' plays on the soundtrack, they kiss.

Original Airdate: 15 February 1999

Sideshow

What's Ally to do now that she and Billy have kissed?

'Backfield in Motion' plays, while Ally consults both Dr Tracy and Renee for advice.

'Sex is physical, sometimes it's primal,' she tells her roommate. 'A raging penis, a burning – oh, never mind!' To Ally's concerns

Renee replies: 'Any relationship starts with dishonesty. It sets the stage for marriage.'

At which point, of course, Dr Greg arrives at the flat. Naturally, he's followed in short order by Billy himself. Ally, who has her therapist on speed dial for just such occasions, pushes both suitors out, blithering all the while.

Dr Tracy is her usual astringent self, sneeringly calling Ally a 'baby' and a 'slut'. Of Billy, Ally stammers that 'he wants to have his cake and not eat me – it, it!' Tracy's advice: Have sex with Greg. . .or should it be Billy?

Ally and Billy challenge each other to meet for an assignation, but can't go through with it: they just kiss, once, and a single tear courses down Ally's cheek.

How guilty does Ally feel now? Back in the office, she even has a vision of Georgia walking around with a knife sticking out of her back. And in the office Elaine calls Ally and Billy 'snap' and 'ish'. Later, Dr Tracy sees both Ally and Billy, telling them it's been eleven years, three months and two days since she lost her own true love. Later, she launches into a spirited rendition of 'Tainted Love'.

Billy is incredulous: 'This is the person nurturing your mental health?' he asks Ally. Tracy places Ally's hand in Billy's and has them close their eyes and imagine growing old together, just as Ally once had Whipper imagine growing old with the man of her dreams. 'Consider this and only this,' Tracy says, putting their hands together. 'Is this the picture or not?'

When Billy describes Ally as having had plastic surgery done to her face, Ally protests – in another wry joke with wider-world echoes: 'These are my real lips! I'm good-looking by nature!'

'Love is wasted on you,' says Billy, wounding Ally deeply as their argument escalates, 'because you'll always be unhappy.'

Tearful, crushed, Ally tells him she loves him . . . and then says goodbye.

Original Airdate: 22 February 1999

Sex, Lies and Politics

Cage and Ling represent a bookstore owner who was driven out of business by a senator who claimed the store sold pornography, while Ally and Billy deal with the aftermath of their kiss, which includes Ally imagining that strangers on the street are talking about it and that Georgia's head is beating like some tell-tale heart.

Later, Ally even apologizes to Greg for kissing another man and goes to church to be forgiven, but ends up arguing with the minister who says that breaking the 'Thou shalt not commit adultery' commandment is the worst of all. 'What about the prohibition against murder?' Ally protests. Still later, Ally phones Dr Ruth's radio talk show for advice.

Meanwhile, Billy has blurted out to Georgia that he kissed Ally and Georgia tells him they should separate for a while.

In court, Ling's closing argument – that suing a politician because of his opinions is 'stupid', but that this particular politico exploited the bookstore for publicity and drove it out of business – sways the jury and the bookstore owner wins over a million dollars in damages.

Ally approaches Georgia and tries to explain that although she and Billy love one another, they were never meant to be together. Georgia asks her to leave.

Original Airdate: 1 March 1999

Civil Wars

It's a double-team grudge match when Ally and Cage face off against Fish and Georgia in a date-rape case, while Nelle, who has a phobia about perspiration, represents a sweaty client in trouble with the Internal Revenue Service.

Over end-of-the-day drinks, Billy admits to Fish and Cage that he and Ally kissed. Naturally, Fish wants him to describe, in detail, Ally's tongue.

The son of an important client is being sued for date rape, with Ally representing the plaintiff, so Fish arranges for the firm to represent both sides. How cute is the defendant, Renee wants to know later. Ally replies without hesitation: 'Spanky toy'.

In court, Paula, Ally and Cage's client, describes how she met Kevin, Fish and Georgia's client, at a party. After they dated and made love, he revealed that he impersonated a woman in an online chat room so he could learn her likes and dislikes. To Ally, Georgia's cross-examination comment, that people sometimes cheat in a relationship, seems aimed at her and she objects. On the stand Kevin says he was too timid to approach Paula without inside knowledge.

In court, the epic Cage versus Fish battle turns sharp indeed. 'Got into her chatroom,' Cage says of the boy Fish and Georgia are defending, 'got into her pants'.

'Venus, Mars,' Fish retorts succinctly. 'Men are sometimes misguided by a different missile.'

But the only winners in the great Cage/Fish showdown are the clients. The two young people, impressed by their lawyers' arguments, opt for a settlement and a renewed courtship. Grumbles Fish: 'We can't take a contingency on bliss.'

In the tax case, Ling pronounces 'Yucky doo', meeting the sweaty fat man. Blocking his extended hand with a book held protectively in front of herself, she adds blithely, 'That's Chinese for hello.' Later, Ling encourages Nelle to let down her hair and use her feminine wiles with the tax examiner, which, of course, works.

We've already seen a fantasy sequence in which Georgia and Ally turned into snarling cats. We've already heard Georgia say sarcastically that, because she considers Ally a 'friend', as her opponent in court it will be easier to think of Ally as the 'conniving backstabber who kissed my husband'. Now, in the unisex bathroom, they fight for real, with Ling and Nelle joining in. Billy,

Fish and Cage pull the combatants apart and Ally heads for the emergency room, with a cut above her eye, where she learns that Paula and Kevin have reconciled and Dr Greg, whom Ally has been guiltily avoiding, gives her a painful tetanus shot.

Original Airdate: 5 April 1999

Those Lips, That Hand

Who can judge mad love? Ally defends a man accused of murdering his beloved wife by cutting off her hand and Billy and Georgia represent a life insurance salesman who's lost his job because of his love for his bad comb-over.

But what really concerns self-absorbed Ally, with her twenty-ninth birthday approaching, is not the impending murder trial, but the new wrinkle that has appeared on her face. 'All I got out of my last relationship is a tetanus shot,' Ally moans to Renee.

Meanwhile, Richard is threatening to break up with Ling because she won't have 'old-fashioned premarital intercourse'.

Frustrated, Richard goes to the office expert for advice, the self-deprecating Elaine, who explains that women are different. She, for example, is easy: 'I'd sleep with you if you want', she says with a shrug and smile. Clearly it's not an offer that Richard, besotted by Ling's finger-licking ways, hears, much less takes up.

'It must be hard being human', Ling sighs when Richard confronts her with his break-up threat. 'I wouldn't know because I haven't tried it.' Then she rekindles his ardour, and literally drives him to his knees, by licking his finger, letting him stroke her upraised throat and wafting her hair over his face. Later, Ling tells Richard that he'd go blind if she made love to him – she's that good – but Richard recoups afterward with his own maddenly masterful seduction trick: the irresistible knee-pit stroke.

In the murder trial, a policeman describes how he discovered a severed human hand in Ally and Cage's client's car, and how at the client's home officers discovered the body of his wife.

Ally and Cage theorize that the hand was cut off after the wife died of a heart attack, and even well-known media-therapist Dr Joyce Brothers turns up to testify that the loss of a loved one can trigger psychotic behaviour.

Cage's squeaky shoes set Renee off on a round of strenuous objections, and she retaliates with her own theatrical trick, suddenly turning on a power saw in court.

The defendant testifies that he would often sit by his wife's side and hold her hand, and that after she died the thought of never being able to hold her hand again seemed unbearable. He, quite literally, wanted to hold on to her, even after her death.

Meanwhile, in the comb-over case, Billy and Georgia's client is claiming age discrimination, but his ex-boss says the problem is that the salesman's hair might drive prospective clients away, because they can't trust a man with a 'fraudulent' comb-over. While 'Let's Hang On to What We've Got' plays, the lawyers pull the salesman's long strands of hair. Later, in a settlement, the salesman gets his job back in return for a new, non-fraudulent haircut and Ling marches in – to the accompaniment of the Wicked Witch theme from *The Wizard of Oz* – and gives him a few quick snips. Comb-over gone, case closed.

Back at the murder trial, John tells Ally that Nelle suspects that he's in love with. . .Ally.

In closing arguments Renee argues that 'sometimes how it looks is exactly how it is', but Ally counters that only mad love can explain her client's mad action and the jury is swayed. Not guilty.

'Would it be pushing things to try to get her hand back?' the relieved defendant asks after the verdict and Ally assures him it would.

Then Cage, who is about to turn thirty-five, has his own little mad moment, suddenly kissing Renee on the lips. 'Life is for the living', he tells her. 'I like it.'

During the double birthday celebration at the bar, Elaine sings a rousing 'My Pledge of Love', and Nelle surprises Cage with the best birthday present ever: a live performance by Barry White. Open-mouthed with disbelief, Cage goes dancing jerkily up to his idol, with the entire cast following him up and ending the episode with a nicely choreographed line dance.

Original Airdate: 19 April 1999

Let's Dance

While Cage, Fish and Nelle defend a law firm charged with denying a partnership to a female attorney who became pregnant, Ling substitutes for Elaine's partner in a dance contest and Billy and Georgia attend therapy.

When the female attorney, Marianne, takes the stand she says that, like herself, six other female attorneys at the firm were denied partnerships after taking leaves of absence to have babies. Later, Fish asks one of the other side's experts, a woman whose name is Margaret Camaro, if she's a lesbian. During closing arguments, Nelle argues that the female attorney is seeking special consideration, not equal treatment, but this is another one of the rare times when a jury disagrees with a Cage/Fish argument. They find for the plaintiff.

At Billy and Georgia's session, the therapist tells Billy that if she was his wife she'd 'kick his ass', and asks to meet with Ally as well. When she does, she proceeds to call her 'sucky face'.

Meanwhile Ling – in yet another 'lesbian sight gag' – offers to be Elaine's substitute dance partner and dresses as a man for the competition.

Later, without the abrasive therapist to stir them up, Billy and Georgia approach reconciliation when Billy takes Georgia's hand.

Original Airdate: 26 April 1999

Only the Lonely

Perhaps Richard Fish's unrepentant opinions are beginning to rub off on the otherwise demure Billy Thomas. When Billy, who is representing an employer being sued by a slightly overweight woman claiming the monthly 'beach day' at her office amounted to sexual harassment, belittles the complaint, Ally, Georgia and Nelle are dismayed and disgusted.

Elaine believes her face bra will make her an infomercial millionaire, but then Aunt Gladys, who's applied for a patent on the face bra, files a lawsuit that claims her deceased daughter, Martha, came up with the idea.

Meanwhile, Cage is thinking of using Fish's 'knee pit' manoeuvre, which he's already tried out to spectacular results with Renee, on Nelle. But on Nelle the erotic ploy causes pain, not pleasure, and once again Cage is dismayed.

In court, when Billy's client takes the witness stand to insist that workers clad in bathing suits are not embarrassing or disruptive to the workplace, the other side engages in a distinctly Cage/Fish-like ploy: women in bikinis enter the courtroom, followed by a man wearing speedos. Despite the ploy, and the testimony of a pretty secretary who says she felt pressured to participate and wear a bathing suit, the jury sides with Billy and the firm.

Meanwhile, Elaine produces a videotape made at a birthday years before, on which Martha asks Elaine about her face-bra idea.

Later, Nelle takes Cage, Fish and Ling to a rap club and Cage finally gives her a kiss.

Then Nelle invites Cage to her place for dinner while Ally goes to the hospital to tell Greg how strongly she feels about him. But as she watches unseen, Greg goes out with a date. Meanwhile, Cage adapts the flying dismount he's been practising in the unisex into a flying mount as he flies into bed with Nelle.

Original Airdate: 3 May 1999

The Green Monster

The Green Monster – jealousy – is stalking the denizens of Cage/Fish: Ally hires a male escort, hoping to make Greg jealous, and Billy is bothered by looks Georgia gets when she wears Ling's creation – a revealing dress.

Meanwhile, Fish and Cage are representing Bonnie Mannix, a woman who destroyed her husband's most cherished possessions after she discovered him cheating. Using a crane, she hoisted his beloved baby grand piano and dropped it down on his beloved Porsche.

As it happens, among Ling's many business ventures is an escort service, which she suggests Ally employ to make Dr Greg jealous. The man Ling offers, Kevin, is so handsome Ally immediately has a fantasy about devouring his whole face with a kiss. This special-effects reaction is less than surprising, particularly because we already know that Ally locates her self-esteem, such as it is, in her lips.

Renee convinces Greg to attend John Cage's belated thirty-fifth birthday party, where Ally will be with Kevin, but Greg shows up at the bar with his ultra-beautiful date, Kimba.

The party turns into an occasion for duelling musical numbers – Kevin and Ally singing 'All I Have To Do Is Dream', then Greg and Kimba doing 'Your Precious Love'.

Later, at the jealousy trial, the jury rules in the husband's favour, but awards him damages of only thirty-five cents. Meanwhile Billy, settling his own jealousy case, assures Georgia she doesn't need startling dresses to keep him from being bored and he promises to be better at proving it to her.

Original Airdate: 10 May 1999

Love's Illusions

Is Ally finally losing her mind? Is a man whose wife never loved him, but was a good wife in every other respect, the victim of a fraud? And is something Fish-y going on when Ling finally agrees to make love? They're love's illusions all, including Ally's vivid teenage memory of singing 'Addicted to Love' with her girlfriends.

In court, Ally and Cage represent Kelly, whose husband is suing her after discovering fantasy love letters, some dating back eleven years, in her private diary. While cross-examining the husband, Ally has a hallucination in which the judge leaps up and begins singing an Al Green song. Later, with Kelly on the stand saying that love is 'probably all an illusion', Ally has yet another Al Green soul-music fantasy.

In a stall of the unisex, Georgia and Billy's reminiscences about the single life turn to passion, but as Ally and Cage enter, with Ally telling Cage every marriage needs passion, the stall door flies open and Billy and Georgia, entwined, fall to the floor. Can Elaine, camera at the ready, be far behind?

Meanwhile, Fish is climbing into bed, ready to claim his dream, too – sex with Ling – but. . .

'This is an E-ticket, Richard', she says, making reference to the very best form of amusement-park access, 'with a minimum size requirement to ride', and she thrusts a waiver (which says 'You have no known heart conditions, no history of seizures, no back injuries') and a confidentiality agreement at him, explaining she has to protect her 'trade secrets'.

And when he reluctantly signs, Ling leaps on him, shouting, 'Action!'

But Fish flops, so instead of making love they watch TV, just happening to tune into *Chicago Hope*, another David E. Kelley show. Later, Fish consults a doctor, who prescribes a Viagra-like medication. Still later, Ling relents and gives him a second chance.

This time, to the R&B soundtrack pulse of 'I'm Just a Love Machine', Fish wows her with his chemically enhanced ardour.

Original Airdate: 17 May 1999

I Know Him By Heart

When Renee discovers Ally in the middle of another Al Green musical fantasy, she tells Ally that she's worried about her well-being.

Her heart is a giant stress fracture, Ally says, telling Renee she's going to stay in her room, where her life 'is beautiful'. Later, Ally comes to the conclusion that her dream man doesn't exist and Renee urges Ally to join her in the dating scene.

When Ally finally returns to work, she asks Ling for a make-over. But when she asks Ling to 'do her', Ling thinks it's a come-on, so she tells Ally to stick out her finger. But Ling doesn't actually lick, protesting that she's grossed out by the thought. Later, she tells Fish that she believes Ally is a lesbian.

That night, Ally and Renee hit the clubs and bars, meeting an endless succession of loser men, so Ling offers to bring all the available men in Boston to Ally. Later Ling delivers a parade of handsome, eligible men, but Ally rejects them all.

Nelle tells Cage she's threatened by the way he connects to Ally's fantasy life. Cage then tells Ally that one of the reasons for the connection is that, as a little boy, he pitched an imaginary no-hitter in his own imaginary Little League.

Later, Nelle and Cage discuss their differences and the growing tension between them, and Cage insists that the one non-negotiable thing in their relationship is that Nelle must eventually come to love all things Barry White. Their affection is beginning to deepen into love, and they kiss.

That night, Ally sits alone on a carousel, going around and around.

This is the final episode of the second season. No sooner had it aired than the media criticism began all over again:

Does Ally's near breakdown and despair that she won't ever find the man of her dreams signify that she's gone from being a bad feminist to being no feminist at all? Has she finally turned into a male's hostile vision of the professional woman as depressed, fragile, emotional, naive, unable to go on, and so forth and so on?

Stay tuned.

Original Airdate: 24 May 1999

A Final Word
from the Author

Bygones.

About the Author

Louis Chunovic is the author of more than a dozen books about television and show business, including biographies of Marilyn Monroe, Bruce Lee and Jodie Foster, and has written for both daily Hollywood trade papers and numerous other publications as well.

The only member of the Ally cast he's ever met, however, is Dyan Cannon (Judge 'Whipper' Cone), with whom he once queued up at a health-food store. He's happy to report that in person she was charming and patient and looked absolutely radiant.